GOD SO LOVED...

John 3:16

An Introduction to Christ and Christianity

Steve Ink

WestBow
PRESS®
A DIVISION OF THOMAS NELSON
& ZONDERVAN

WestBow Press books may be ordered through booksellers or by contacting:

WestBow Press
A Division of Thomas Nelson & Zondervan
1663 Liberty Drive
Bloomington, IN 47403
www.westbowpress.com
1 (866) 928-1240

ISBN: 978-1-4908-7689-4 (sc)
ISBN: 978-1-4908-7688-7 (hc)
ISBN: 978-1-4908-7690-0 (e)

Library of Congress Control Number: 2015906211

Print information available on the last page.

WestBow Press rev. date: 11/07/2019

THANKS

To those of you who reviewed the manuscript
and made helpful suggestions for this book.

To my brother, Bruce Ink,
For creating the cover artwork.

www.steveink.net

Contents

Bible Abbreviations

Old Testament

Genesis (Ge)
Exodus (Ex)
Leviticus (Lev)
Numbers (Nu)
Deuteronomy (Dt)
Joshua (Jos)
Judges (Jdg)
Ruth (Ru)
1 Samuel (1Sa)
2 Samuel (2Sa)
1 Kings (1Ki)
2 Kings (2 Ki)
1 Chronicles (1Ch)
2 Chronicles (2Ch)
Ezra (Ezr)
Nehemiah (Ne)
Esther (Est)
Job (Job)
Psalms (Ps)

Ecclesiastes (Ecc)
Song of Songs (SS)
Isaiah (Isa)
Jeremiah (Jer)
Lamentations (La)
Ezekiel (Eze)
Daniel (Da)
Hosea (Hos)
Joel (Joel)
Amos (Am)
Obadiah (Ob)
Jonah (Jnh)
Micah (Mic)
Nahum (Na)
Habakkuk (Hab)
Zephaniah (Zep)
Haggai (Hag)
Zechariah (Zec)
Malachi (Mal)

New Testament

Matthew (Mt)
Mark (Mk)
Luke (Lk)

John (Jn)
Acts (Ac)
Romans (Ro)

1 Corinthians (1Co)   Philemon (Phm)
2 Corinthians (2Co)   Hebrews (Heb)
Galatians (Gal)   James (Jas)
Ephesians (Eph)   1 Peter (1Pe)
Philippians (Php)   2 Peter (2Pe)
Colossians (Col)   1 John (1Jn)
1 Thessalonians (1Th)   2 John (2Jn)
2 Thessalonians (2Th)   3 John (3Jn)
1 Timothy (1Ti)   Jude (Jude)
2 Timothy (2Ti)   Revelation (Rev)
Titus (Tit)

Thus Jn.3:16 references the Bible book "John," Chapter 3, verse 16.

All biblical quotes are taken from the *New International Version*, Quickverse software ver.3.0.0(119), 2009.

Preface

Here He Comes

Everyone knew his name. He had excited the people as no other had. His words were powerful. He was fearless even before the authorities. He had a confidence that exuded from the sense that he knew what he was talking about from first hand experience. He didn't just study about God. He really knew God. The tales of his healings ran rampant throughout Jerusalem.

Just days before, in Bethany, two miles out of Jerusalem, Jesus had stood before a cave, which served as the tomb for the corpse of his friend, Lazarus. Those mourning with the sisters of Lazarus watched Jesus as he prayed to God. Then Jesus shouted, "Lazarus, come out!" Their eyes turned to the cave not sure what to expect. To the astonishment of all who were present, a shrouded body slowly walked out of the darkness of the cave. It was Lazarus – raised after being dead for four days. Could Jesus truly be the long awaited and prophesied messiah? Many ran to Jerusalem and excitedly shared the story of the miracle they had just seen occur.

The religious leaders of the day also took notice of the events of Bethany, but they had a different reaction. Many false messiahs had risen to prominence claiming to be the savior only to be executed by the Roman authorities. These self-proclaimed "messiah's" had given people a false hope. Such a false hope might eventually lead to the destruction of their faith and a rejection of the prophecies and teachings of Scripture. Hoping in someone who is eventually executed without fulfilling his mission is deflating and frustrating. It is faith destroying.

Additionally this itinerant preacher was proclaiming some radical ideas. Jesus taught people were to love their enemies, which was completely impractical and dangerous. He taught that the people should follow God's words from Scripture. He explained the religious leaders were often hypocrites in giving lip service to the teachings and then finding some selfish and self-serving way around the principles of Scripture. Most of all, Jesus was leading the people away from the authoritative ruling of the religious leaders. He had to be stopped. But how?

Then word spread that Jesus was coming to Jerusalem. Crowds started to gather in anticipation at the entrances to the city. The religious leaders also gathered to analyze the situation and develop a plan. Jesus climbed on the back of a donkey and entered town in the company of his Apostles, other disciples, and huge crowds lining the streets. Riding a donkey with followers before an enthusiastic crowd was the long held symbol of a king's processional. This further disturbed the religious leaders.

Jerusalem had not seen anything like this in a long time. The people who lined the streets spread their cloaks on the road before Jesus and began shouting, "Hosanna, Hosanna!" They laid palm branches on the ground before Jesus as a sign of honor much like we lay out the red carpet. The religious leaders were clearly agitated at the excitement Jesus had created. How could so many fall for this charlatan? What could they do to stop him without inciting a mob reaction?

As Jesus rode by one of the religious leaders, the exasperated man of authority commanded Jesus, "Teacher, rebuke your disciples," for they were much too exuberant. Jesus responded, "I tell you, if they keep quiet, the stones will cry out!" This leader got the message. Jesus was saying that just as it is not in the nature of a stone to cry out, it is also not in the nature of a disciple of Christ, excited by the greatest event and personage in the history of mankind, to keep quiet.[1] This was God incarnate passing by. How in the world could you keep those who recognized this quiet?

The raising of Lazarus from the dead and Jesus' triumphal entry into Jerusalem were the final straws. This man had to be stopped and the religious leaders would find a way to do it. Within a few days, this itinerant preacher, this "messiah," would be dead and buried along with all the other "false" messiahs. But that was not the end of the story. As one song powerfully proclaims - it was only the "end of the beginning!"[2]

The Story of Jesus

The story of Jesus is the foundation of Christianity. The name "Christianity" itself comes from the title we give to Jesus "Christ." As such, this book will begin with an introduction to the story of Jesus Christ. For the sake of brevity, many events, and some of the details of the events included, are selectively missing.

The Christian message is really pretty simple. God is holy and cannot tolerate sin in his presence. He created the universe and its life with people being God's creative masterpiece. People sin and that causes a separation between God and his greatest creation. Jesus had to empty himself of his divinity, come to the earth as a man, die on the cross and be resurrected to life to provide the opportunity for forgiveness, reconciliation to God and eternal life to people. We now need to unite with Christ, commit to God's

---

[1] *Not in the nature.* Landon Saunders shared this thought at a keynote speech he gave at the Beautiful Feet Mission Workshop at Abilene Christian University in Abilene, Texas in the early 1970's.

[2] *End of the Beginning,* Music & words written and performed by David Phelps on *The Best of David Phelps* album released Mar.18, 2011, Spring House Music Group, EMI Christian Music Group.

leadership, and allow God to shape us into the people that we can only be with his help.

This is not just a religion. It is not just a philosophy. It is a relationship with the God who came in the form of a man, to walk, teach, model and guide us through the promised abundant life. Jesus is God in the flesh. We see God through Jesus. Forgiveness and life come through Jesus.

> No man ever loved like Jesus. He taught the blind to see and the dumb to speak. He died on the cross to save us. He bore our sins. And now God says, "Because He did, I can forgive you.
>
> *Billy Graham*[3]

Why Write about One Verse in the Bible?

Although we begin with a look at the story of Jesus, this book is based on one single verse of the Bible. Every so often someone utters a statement that is so brief, concise, and powerful that it flames the human imagination. It captures the heart of humankind. Its brevity emotes power. It portrays in a few words a vision of life that others could not duplicate even with ten thousand words. It is so profound that when we read or hear the statement - we stop to contemplate its meaning and force.

You know the types of sayings. "What's in a name? That which we call a rose by any other name would smell as sweet." This phrase was written by William Shakespeare in Romeo and Juliet (A.2,s.2) to illustrate that a family *name* does not make one family better than another.[4] "We hold these truths to be self-evident, that all

---

[3]   *Quotable Quotations*, Compiled by Lloyd Cory, Wheaton, IL: Victor Books, 1985, p.199, *Jesus.*

[4]   *Shakespeare The Complete Works*, Ed by G.B. Harrison, New York, Harcourt, Brace & World, Inc., 1968, p.484.

men are created equal, that they are endowed by their Creator with certain unalienable Rights, that among these are Life, Liberty, and the pursuit of Happiness."[5] These words were drafted by Thomas Jefferson for the Declaration of Independence in 1776 to lay out the rationale for separation from England. Franklin D. Roosevelt uttered, "The only thing we have to fear is fear itself" on March 4, 1933 to encourage a nation devastated by the Great Depression.[6] "Ask not what your country can do for you, ask what you can do for your country,"[7] was spoken by John F. Kennedy at his January 20, 1961 Inauguration to encourage a spirit of service. Martin Luther King, Jr. preached "I have a dream," at the steps of the Lincoln Memorial on August 28, 1963 to help people visualize a nation without racial prejudice.[8] "It ain't over 'til it's over" was uttered by Yogi Berra on September 26, 1977 when the Mets were nine games out of first place to illustrate the fact that you can't count someone out until the very end.[9] The Mets won the division title that season. All of these sayings were concise, clear, and powerful.

The Gettysburg Address is a great example of a powerful thought captured in just a few words. After the ferocious battle of Gettysburg, Pennsylvania in July 1863, a national cemetery was established to provide an honored place for the dead. Edward Everett, a distinguished statesman and famous orator, gave the keynote address. President Abraham Lincoln was invited as an afterthought. Everett spoke for more than two hours. Lincoln spoke for about two minutes. A century and a half later, we remember the words of Lincoln, not Everett. This moving two-minute speech begins with these famous words,

---

5   *The Yale Book of Quotations*, ed by Fred R. Shapiro, New Haven & London: Yale University Press, 2006, p.391, Thomas Jefferson §2.
6   *Ibid*, Franklin Roosevelt, p.645, §6.
7   *Ibid*, John Kennedy, p.421, §16.
8   *Ibid*, Martin Luther King, Jr., p.427, §3.
9   *Ibid*, Yogi Berra, p.58, §12.

Four score and seven years ago our fathers brought forth on this continent a new nation, conceived in liberty, and dedicated to the proposition that all men are created equal. Now we are engaged in a great civil war, testing whether that nation, or any nation, so conceived and so dedicated, can long endure. ...[10]

These short, moving phrases, developed by the genius of people or the inspiration of God, raise the human spirit.

John 3:16

I have chosen in this book to write about one of these simple yet profound phrases. It is found in the Bible and commonly known as John 3:16. The phrase was originally written in the late 1st century AD in Greek and would have looked something like this,

ΟΥΤΩΣΥΑΡΗΓΑΠΗΣΕΝΟΘΕΟΣΤΟΝΚΟΣΜΟΝΩ
ΣΤΕΤΟΝΥΙΟΝΤΟΝΜΟΝΟΓΕΝΗΕΔΩΚΕΝ
ΙΝΑΠΑΣΟΠΙΣΤΕΥΩΝΕΙΣΑΥΤΟΝΜΗΑΠΟ
ΛΤΑΙΑΛΛΕΧΗΖΩΗΝΑΙΩΝΙΟΝ[11]

It has been translated into modern English as,

---

[10] *Famous Statements Speeches & Stories of Abraham Lincoln*, Ed & published by J. Donal Hawkins, 1991, p.53.

[11] *Ancient wording.* In modern Greek depiction it would look like this: ουτως γαρ ηγαπησεν ο θεος τον κοσμον ωστε τον υιον τον μονογενη εδωκεν ινα πας ο πιστευων εις αυτον μη αποληται αλλ εχη ζωην αιωνιον. *The Greek New Testament*, 3rd Ed., by Aland, Kurt; Black, Matthew; Martini, Carlo M.; Metzger, Bruce M.; Wikgren, & Allen, Editors, West Germany: United Bible Societies, 1983, p.330.

*For God so loved the world, that he gave his one and only
Son, that whoever believes in him shall not perish but have
everlasting life.*[12]

Why Write About This Verse?

Of all the thousands of verses in the Bible, John 3:16 is a favorite.
It is a favorite because it gets at the heart of the Gospel message in
one potent sentence. One could dwell and meditate for a lifetime
on this one sentence and each day dig deeper and deeper into its
meaning. Each day could bring new and fuller understanding of
who God is, who man is, and what God has done to save man from
sin and himself. I love this verse – just as much as the world does.

This verse is really a map through the message of Christianity.
It can be used as a guide to talk about the Christian message. It may
not address all the issues that would be laid out in a systematic
presentation of Christianity, but it hits all the salient parts of the
Good News of Jesus Christ. This is probably why this passage is so
popular.

What People Say

Many great authors have seen the power in this succinct verse.

---

[12] *New International Version*, Quickverse software ver.3.0.0(119), 2009, John
3:16. All biblical quotes in this book come from the New International
Version. I chose this version because it is deemed a type of "dynamic
equivalent" of the original Hebrew and Greek that finds the middle ground
between literal word for word translations (which seek to preserve the
original terminology but is often awkward), and paraphrases (which seek
to communicate in today's modern English but sometimes strays from
the original terminology). *The Challenge of Bible Translation*, by Glen G.
Scorgie, Mark L. Strauss, & Steven M. Voth, Grand Rapids, MI: Zondervan,
2003, p.53.

We have now arrived at the great metropolis of gospel truth. No other single statement in the Bible so aptly sums up God's redemptive purpose in Christ for the human race. Volumes have been written on it. Its each and every word has been weighted and examined and marveled at and preached on. Who will ever know until the judgment seat of Christ how many millions of Adam's ruined race have found their way to heaven by the discovery of John 3:16?

John Phillips[13]

The Hope diamond of the Bible... A twenty-six-word parade of hope: beginning with God, ending with life, and urging us to do the same. Brief enough to write on a napkin or memorize in a moment, yet solid enough to weather two thousand years of storms and questions. If you know nothing of the Bible, start here. If you know everything in the Bible, return here. We all need the reminder. The heart of the human problem is the heart of the human. And God's treatment is prescribed in John 3:16.

Max Lucado[14]

John 3:16 (chapter 3, verse 16 of the Gospel of John) is one of the most widely quoted verses from the Christian Bible, and has been called the most famous Bible verse. It has also been called the "Gospel in a nutshell" because it is considered a summary of the central dogma of traditional Christianity. ... The phrase "John 3:16" is very short and can be written inconspicuously in out-of-the-way

---

[13] *Exploring the Gospel of John* by John Phillips, Grand Rapids, MI: Kregel Publications, 1989, p.71.

[14] *The 3:16 Promise*, by Max Lucado, Nashville, TN: Thomas Nelson, 2007, p.1-2.

locations. In the U.S., the In-N-Out Burger chain prints it on the inside of the bottom rim of their paper cups, clothing chain Forever 21 and Heritage (1981) print it on the bottom of their shopping bags, and Tornado Fuel Saver prints it on the box.

Wikipedia[15]

Let God

As you read this book and study this powerful verse, allow God to speak to you. Listen for his voice. Look for his teaching. Let God's Spirit fill you with the wonder that will undoubtedly arise as you spend more time with this profound statement of spiritual truth.

---

[15] *John 3:16*, online at http://en.wikipedia.org/wiki/John_3:16.

1

The Greatest Story Ever Told

The four gospels of the New Testament - Matthew, Mark, Luke and John – tell the story of Jesus. Matthew and John were disciples of Jesus and knew him well. Mark and Luke learned about Jesus from those who were eyewitnesses. To fully understand John 3:16, to which we will turn our attention in the following chapters, it is helpful to know something about the story of Jesus. This story has been called, "the greatest story ever told." After looking at its impact on the world for the past two thousand years, it would be difficult to argue with this assessment.[1]

Pronouncing Jesus' Birth

During the end of the last century BC, the Jews held great expectation that God would send a Messiah (aka Christ)[2] to restore

---

[1]   *The story of Jesus* is told here chronologically as laid out by Robert L. Thomas and Stanley N. Gundry in *The NIV Harmony of the Gospels*, New York, NY: Harper Collins Publishers, 1988. This is an abbreviated version of the story from the four Gospels. Many events are left out for the sake of brevity.

[2]   *Messiah* comes from משיח meaning "anointed one" referring to a king chosen by God. *The New Strong's Expanded Dictionary of Bible Words*, by James Strong, Nashville, TN: Thomas Nelson Publishers, 2001, p.639, §4899. The Greek translation of this term is χριστος (*christos*) transliterated as "Christ." p.1458, §5547. We commonly think of the Messiah or Christ as "savior."

the Kingdom of David from old. He would be the savior of the world. Old Testament prophecies pointed to this coming Messiah.[3] The Jews were tired of the overbearing pagan rule of the Roman Empire. Every so often someone would arise and proclaim himself Messiah, gather a following, and then be executed by the authorities. This did not dampen the people's hope or expectation. The Jews longed for the relief that would accompany God's coming Messiah.

Somewhere in the gap between 7 BC and 4 BC, during the time of King Herod of Judea, the angel Gabriel visited Mary, who may have been a young teenager. Mary lived in the town of Nazareth in Galilee in the present Middle East. This was a small rural agricultural town of probably no more than 500 residents located about 63 miles north of Jerusalem.[4] Gabriel told Mary that she would have a child and he would be named "Jesus." Mary questioned how this could occur, as she was still a virgin. Mary was pledged to be married to Joseph, a carpenter,[5] but she remained in a separate house without

---

[3] *Prophecies of Jesus.* Ge.3:15=Ga.4:4; Ge.18:18=Ac.3:25; Ge.17:19=Mt.1:2; Nu.24:17=Lk.3:34; Ge.49:10=Lk.3:33; Isa.9:7=Mt.1:1; Mic.5:2=Mt.2:1; Da.9:25=Lk.2:1-2; Isa.7:14=Mt.1:18; Jer.31:15=Mt.2:16; Hos.11:1=Mt.2:14; Isa.9:1-2=Mt.4:12-16; Dt.18:15=Jn.6:14; Ps.110:4=Heb.6:20; Isa.53:3=Jn.1:11; Isa.11:2=Lk.2:52; Zec.9:9=Jn.12:13-14; Ps.41:9=Mt.14:10; Zec.11:12=Mt.26:15; Zec.11:13=Mt.27:6-7; Ps.109:7-8=Ac.1:18-20; Ps.27:12=Mt.26:60-61; Isa.53:7=Mt.26:62-63; Isa.50:6=Mt.14:65; Ps.69:4=Jn.15:23-25; Isa.53:4-5=Mt.8:16-17; Isa.53:12=Mt.27:38; Ps.22:16=Jn.20:27; Ps.22:6-8=Mt.27:39-40; Ps.69:21=Jn.19:29; Ps.22:8=Mt.27:43; Ps.109:4=Lk.23:34; Zec.12:10=Jn.19:34=Ps.22:18=Mk.15:24; Ps.34:20=Jn.19:33; Isa.53:9=Mt.27:57-60; Ps.16:10=Mt.28:9; Ps.68:18=Lk.24:50-51. List found in *The Thompson Chain-Reference Bible,* Indianapolis, IN: B.B. Kirkbride Bible Co., Inc., 1990, p.1703-1706.

[4] *Nazareth,* online at http://en.wikipedia.org/wiki/Nazareth; *Nazareth Israel History,* online at http://www.nazareth-israel.com/nazarteh-history; *Distance from Jerusalem to Nazareth,* online at http://www.distancefromto.net/between/Jerusalem/Nazareth

[5] *Carpentry.* Mt.13:55. Carpentry could have included building houses, furniture, cabinets, carts, or virtually anything made of wood. Nazareth was a rather small town for a full time carpentry profession, but there

sexual contact. The angel explained that the Holy Spirit would come upon her and God's power would impregnate her. Mary faithfully accepted what the angel had told her.[6]

By this custom of the day being "pledged" meant Joseph and Mary were bound to each other as if married except that they still lived in separate houses and were not engaged sexually. It would have taken a divorce to break the bond. When Mary returned from a three-month visit to her relative, Elizabeth, her pregnancy was discovered. Joseph, not wanting to disgrace Mary, planned to divorce Mary quietly. But then an angel appeared to him in a dream and helped Joseph understand that the baby was conceived by the Holy Spirit, and not by another man. Upon awakening, Joseph took Mary as his wife, but had no sexual union with her until after she had given birth to Jesus.[7]

Jesus' Birth

Caesar Augustus, the nephew of Julius Caesar who defeated Mark Antony and Cleopatra, known as the first Roman Emperor, ordered that a census be taken of the entire Roman Empire at the time Mary was still pregnant.[8] Every man and his family were to go to

---

are any number of explanations that could easily have made carpentry a reasonable profession here. (a) Poor people needed very little to survive in a small town. (b) It is possible that carpentry was a skill that supplemented his own growing of food. (c) Joseph may have used his skill for products sold in neighboring towns. He may have even traveled to neighboring towns for days, weeks or longer to use his carpentry skill beyond the borders of Nazareth.

[6] Lk.1:26-38.

[7] Mt.1:18-25.

[8] *Census.* Questions have arisen in Luke's description of the census that brought Joseph and Mary to Bethlehem for the birth of Jesus because Quirinius is named as governor at the time in Luke and we know Quirinius was not officially governor until after Jesus' birth. Most scholars today believe Jesus was born between 7-4 BC. Josephus references a census

the man's ancestral town to register. Joseph, who belonged to the line of David, needed to go to Bethlehem. Bethlehem was about 6 miles south of Jerusalem[9] with a notable history. In or about the 19th century BC, Jacob's wife, Rachel, was buried in Bethlehem.[10] In or about the 13th century BC, Naomi brought her daughter-in-law, Ruth, to Bethlehem.[11] Around 1000 BC, Ruth's great grandson, King David, was raised in Bethlehem.[12] About 7-4 BC, Joseph took Mary and started out for Bethlehem to register for the census.

Joseph and Mary probably passed through Jerusalem towards the end of their journey to get to Bethlehem. Melchizedek, Priest of the God Most High had come from this place to visit Abraham around 2000 BC.[13] This is the traditional site upon which Abraham almost sacrificed his son Isaac.[14] A thousand years later King David established Jerusalem as the capital of Israel.[15] Another thousand years later, in Jesus' day, it had a busy population of about 80,000, which swelled during the times of religious festivals.[16] It was built

---

taken about AD 6 when Quirinius was officially governor of Syria (*Antiquities* 17.3.5). Luke 2:2 references an earlier census taken about 7-4 BC when Quirinius was Legate (military general) and *acting* governor of Syria. Luke writes about "the first census" implying there were at least two during the time of Quirinius' leadership in Syria. Quirinius may have conducted both censuses for Rome. The fact that Luke knew about the Roman custom of taking a census every 10-12 years, which was not done 100 years later, and knew about Quirinius, is evidence of the authenticity of the story. *The International Standard Bible Encyclopaedia*, Grand Rapids, MI: Wm.B. Eerdmans Publishing Co., 1980, Vol.I, p.645, *Chronology of Jesus.*

[9] *Bethlehem Then & Now*, by *Rev. Dr. Mitri Raheb* online at http://www.redletterchristians.org/bethlehem-then-and-now/.

[10] Ge.35:19.

[11] Ru.1:19.

[12] 1Sa.16:1-13.

[13] Ge.14:18-20.

[14] Ge.22:1-19.

[15] 2Sa.5:6-16.

[16] *Population of Jerusalem.* Josephus estimated the 1st century population at about 80,000, which then swelled during religious festivals.

on a hill with the magnificent Jewish Temple standing high above all other buildings and dominating the hill and city. At the time of our story, the Temple grounds were undergoing a major renovation. The city was undoubtedly filled with activity.

Upon arriving in Bethlehem, a town of about 1,000 residents,[17] Mary came due. They were forced to take shelter in a stable where animals stayed because there was no room for them in the inn. Jesus was placed in a manger, which is a feeding trough for animals.[18] Traditionally, the place of Jesus' birth was a cave stable without the conveniences of a typical home of the day.

There were shepherds tending sheep in the fields nearby when an angel appeared to them and announced the good news that a savior had been born and that they could find him wrapped in cloths and lying in a manger. As soon as the angels left, the shepherds made their way off to the place where the new baby Jesus was awaking to physical life. After seeing the child themselves, they returned glorifying and praising God for what they had heard and seen.[19]

Far off in distant lands to the East, wise men, called "magi," saw an unusually bright star that they concluded was a sign of the prophesied Messiah. They began the long journey of following the star west. Traditionally the wise men are said to have come from Persia, a considerable distance away.[20] When they arrived in Jerusalem, they asked around if anyone knew the location of the one

---

Tacitus, the Roman, estimated it to be about 600,000. *Demographic History of Jerusalem*, online at http://en.wikipedia.org/wiki/Demographic_history_of_Jerusalem.

[17] *Bethlehem Then & Now, Ibid.*

[18] Lk.2:1-7. Justin Martyr wrote that Jesus was born in a cave (AD 150). Origen also mentions this (AD 250). Queen Helena, wife of Constantine, built a church on what was thought to be the cave of the nativity (AD 325).

[19] Lk.2:8-20.

[20] *Wise men from Persia. Archaeological Study Bible*, Grand Rapids, MI: Zondervan, note 2:1, 2005, p.1560. *The Apologetics Study Bible*, Nashville, TN: Holman Bible Publishing, 2003, p.1405. "Clement of Alexandria, Diodorus of Tarsus, Chrysostom, Cyril of Alexandria, Juvencus, Prudentius and other are probably right in bringing them from Persia."

who had been born king of the Jews. King Herod was a ruthless local king who executed several family members upon suspicion that they were after his crown. No rival kings were permitted to live in this kingdom. When King Herod learned of the inquiry by the wise men, he asked his chief priests and teachers of the law where the Christ (the Messiah) was to be born. The priests and teachers of the law referenced Micah 5:2 in the Old Testament Scripture which pointed to Bethlehem of Judea. King Herod asked the wise men to bring back word of the Messiah's location once they found him so he too could worship the king of the Jews. This was simply a ruse to learn of the baby's location to enable King Herod to execute a rival king.

Upon finding Joseph, Mary and the child in a house, the wise men bowed down and worshipped the young King of Kings. They presented him with gifts of gold, incense and myrrh. Having been warned in a dream, they did not go back and share what they found with King Herod.[21] When King Herod learned the wise men had left without returning with word of the child's location, he gave orders to kill all the boys of Bethlehem who were 2 years old or less. Joseph was warned in a dream and Joseph, Mary and baby Jesus set out for Egypt just before the soldiers came and massacred the young boys of the town.[22] Later, upon learning that King Herod had died, the three pilgrims returned to Nazareth.[23]

Preparing for Ministry

In or about AD 26 John began preaching in the Desert of Judea saying, "Repent, for the Kingdom of heaven is near!" This was the son of Zechariah and Elizabeth whom Mary had gone to visit when

---

The International Standard Bible Encyclopaedia, Grand Rapids, MI: Wm. B. Eerdmans Publishing, 1956, Vol.3, *Magi,* p.1962.

[21] Mt.2:1-12.

[22] Mt.2:13-18.

[23] Mt.2:19-23.

she was first pregnant. John was a strange desert creature wearing clothes made of camel's hair and a leather belt, eating locusts and wild honey. He was commonly called, "John the Baptist," because he would baptize people in the Jordan River as a sign of spiritual cleansing and preparation for the coming Kingdom. John predicted the coming of one more powerful than he, who would baptize people with the Holy Spirit and with fire.[24]

At about age thirty, Jesus came to John at the River Jordan to be baptized by John. John saw Jesus and tried to stop him saying, "I need to be baptized by you, and do you come to me?" But Jesus explained he needed to be baptized "to fulfill all righteousness." So John baptized Jesus and when Jesus came up out of the water, heaven opened and John saw the Spirit of God descending like a dove and lighting on Jesus. John then heard the proud voice of a father as God proclaimed, "This is my Son, whom I love; with him I am well pleased."[25]

Jesus was then led by the Spirit into the desert to be tempted by the devil. For forty days Jesus fasted and he was hungry. The devil came to tempt Jesus when he was most vulnerable. He tried to entice Jesus to perform some miracle to relieve his hunger, but Jesus repeatedly refused the enticement and responded with the words of God from the Old Testament Scripture until the devil finally left.[26]

Jesus' Introduction

Jesus returned to the River Jordan and John identified Jesus as the "Lamb of God" to two of John's disciples. These two disciples left John and followed Jesus. One of the two was Andrew, who went and got his brother, Simon, excitedly exclaiming that Jesus was the "Messiah." Jesus gave Simon the name "Peter," which means "stone"

---

[24] Mt.3:1-12; Mk.1:2-8; Lk.3:3-18.
[25] Mt.3:13-17; Mk.1:9-11; Lk.3:21-23.
[26] Mt.4:1-11; Mk.1:12-13; Lk.4:1-13.

in the Greek, knowing he would be a spiritual rock. Followers were beginning to come.[27]

Jesus went to Jerusalem during a Jewish Passover and found the temple courts filled with the selling of cattle, sheep, and doves for ritualistic sacrifices to God. Others were exchanging money from foreign lands to be used to purchase sacrifices or make offerings. When Jesus saw what was going on he made a whip, released the doves, overturned the moneychanger tables, and chased the marketers out of the temple court. Jesus shouted, "Get these out of here! How dare you turn my Father's house into a market!"[28]

Reaching the Common People

Fisherman on the Sea of Galilee fished at night because the typical haul was better than during the day. Once Andrew and Peter were fishing at night and unable to catch any fish. In the morning Jesus came to the water's edge to preach to the people while the fishermen mended their nets. After Jesus spoke to the people he turned to Peter and encouraged him to put out to sea. Peter knew it was hopeless, but did so anyway. He soon caught so many fish that his net was tearing. Realizing that Jesus was a man of God, he fell at Jesus' knees and said, "Go away from me, Lord: I am a sinful man." Jesus responded, "Don't be afraid; from now on you will catch men."[29]

Jesus went to Capernaum and attended the synagogue on the Sabbath as was his custom and he began to teach. The people were used to rabbis who taught as educated commentators of the Scripture, quoting others to build support for a theological position. Jesus taught as one with the authority that comes with having been there and knowing first hand the truth of the matter. The people

---

[27] Jn.1:35-51.

[28] Jn.2:13-22.

[29] Lk.5:1-11.

were amazed. A man with an evil spirit cried out. Jesus commanded him to "Be quiet!" The man shook violently and then calmed as the evil spirit left him. The people witnessed both the authority in speaking and the casting out of the evil spirit and asked each other, "What is this?" The news about Jesus spread throughout the area.[30]

Jesus went throughout Galilee teaching and preaching about the good news of the Kingdom of God and healing every disease and sickness. He is repeatedly described as having compassion on the people around him.[31] His reputation spread and people began bringing the sick and suffering to him for healing. Crowds were growing.[32]

An Unlikely Disciple

The Romans often hired local people to collect taxes. The tax collectors would be required to charge a minimum to be turned over to the Romans and then add on their own commission. Some tax collectors made good money on the "commission" they charged for collecting the taxes. All the locals hated them. It was even worse when a *Jew* collected taxes. The local Jews saw him as a traitor because the Romans were viewed as the evil pagan government that would one day be overthrown by the coming Messiah. No Jewish religious leader would have anything to do with a tax collector. Matthew, aka Levi, the son of Alphaeus, was a Jewish tax collector. Jesus called Matthew. The tax collector left his practice and followed Jesus.[33]

Matthew then held a great banquet for Jesus at his house and invited his fellow tax collectors and others the religious leaders would label "sinners." The Pharisees were appalled and questioned

---

[30] Mk.1:21-28; Lk.4:31-37.
[31] Mt.9:36; 14:14; 15:32; 20:34; Mk.1:41; 6:34; 8:2.
[32] Mt.4:23-25; Mk.1:35-39; Lk.4:42-44.
[33] Mt.9:9; Mk.2:13-14; Lk.5:27-28.

Jesus' disciples asking how a religious teacher could eat with such people. Jesus heard the questioning and answered, "It is not the healthy who need a doctor, but the sick. ...For I have come not to call the righteous, but sinners to repentance."[34]

Over and over again Jesus upset the Jewish religious leaders by doing the forbidden on the Sabbath (Friday sundown to Saturday sundown). He picked left over grain from farmer's fields for food as the poor were permitted to do. He taught and healed. But he undertook these actions on the Sabbath. Jesus tried to explain that the ritual laws were there to help, but should not take precedence over need. Additionally, identifying himself as "the Son of Man," he explained that, "the Son of Man is Lord of the Sabbath" and therefore the Sabbath law had no authority over Jesus.[35]

Shaping a Team of Leaders

After spending time with those who followed him, Jesus spent all night long praying on a mountainside. In the morning he announced that he had chosen twelve men to serve as his special disciples, who came to be known as the Twelve Apostles. This group was comprised of (1) Simon, named Peter; (2) his brother, Andrew, (3) James and (4) John, the sons of Zebedee, (5) Philip, (6) Bartholomew, aka Nathanael, (7) Matthew, aka Levi, (8) Thomas, aka Didymus, (9) James son of Alpheus, (10) Simon, called the Zealot, (11) Judas son of James, aka Thaddeus, and (12) Judas Iscariot.[36] These are the twelve men who would travel and live with Jesus and, with the exception of Judas Iscariot, would become the early leaders of the Church after Jesus was gone.

Jesus then sat down on the mountainside and began to teach the crowds.

---

[34] Mt.9:10-13; Mk.2:15-17; Lk.5:29-32.
[35] Mt.12:1-14; Mk.2:23-3:6; Lk.6:1-11.
[36] Mk.3:13-19; Lk.6:12-16.

"Blessed are the poor in spirit, for theirs is the kingdom of heaven. Blessed are those who mourn, for they will be comforted. Blessed are the meek, for they will inherit the earth. Blessed are those who hunger and thirst for righteousness, for they will be filled. Blessed are the merciful, for they will be shown mercy. Blessed are the pure in heart, for they will see God. Blessed are the peacemakers, for they will be called sons of God. Blessed are those who are persecuted because of righteousness for theirs is the kingdom of heaven."[37]

He taught that it is not just the outward actions that are important. It is the inner attitude that shapes the outward action. Sin is not just the physical action, but also the misguided heart that directs the outward action. He walked through the common teachings about sin and showed how one must address the attitude behind the outward action. He took a revolutionary step and exhorted his hearers to, "Love your enemies, do good to those who hate you, bless those who curse you, pray for those you mistreat you."[38] Jesus' teaching was different and exciting.

Jesus warned about false prophets who appear righteous, but actually deceive. The way one determines whether someone is a false teacher or prophet is by looking at the fruit of that teacher's life. The teacher's actions show what is truly in his or her heart. Jesus said, "Not everyone who says to me, 'Lord, Lord,' will enter the kingdom of heaven, but only he who does the will of my Father who is in heaven."[39]

He gave encouragement to those who were beaten down by oppressors and hardship. "Ask and it will be given to you; seek and

---

[37] Mt.5:3-12; Lk.6:20-26.
[38] Mt.5:21-48; Lk.6:27-36.
[39] Mt.7:21.

you will find; knock and the door will be opened to you." "Do to others as you would have them do to you."[40]

Jesus traveled with the Twelve, and also a group of women, who helped support him financially. These women included Mary Magdalene, who had been demon possessed until Jesus drove the demons out, Joanna, the wife of the manager of Herod's household, Susanna, and many others.[41]

As an itinerate preacher, Jesus often spoke in parables to describe the nature of the Kingdom of God. A "parable" is a short fictional story about situations common to the people told to illustrate a spiritual truth. Jesus spoke of a farmer sowing seed on various types of soil with varying results of growth to illustrate that each person needs to provide a soft heart to God so that God's word may successfully take root, grow and shape that heart.[42] Jesus told a parable about a farmer who sowed good seed in his field, but an enemy planted weeds at night that looked much like the wheat, to illustrate that we do not have the ability or the authority to identify or to judge bad people or to determine their ultimate value. Judgment is God's business.[43]

The Divine Power of Jesus

Storms can arise quickly on the Sea of Galilee. One day Jesus was in a boat with his disciples. Exhausted from the heavy schedule of teaching and healing, Jesus lay down and fell fast asleep. A storm arose which endangered the boat and frightened the other disciples. When they shouted and awoke him, he saw the waves and the fear of the disciples. Jesus rebuked the winds and the waves saying, "Quiet! Be still!" The winds and waves died down and the

---

[40] Mt.7:7-27; Lk.6:31-49.
[41] Lk.8:1-3.
[42] Mt.13:3-23; Mk.4:3-25; Lk.8:5-18.
[43] Mt.13:24-30, 36-43.

sea grew calm. The terrified disciples looked at Jesus and asked, "Who is this? Even the winds and the waves obey him!"[44]

Once a crowd of about 5,000 or more gathered in the countryside to listen to Jesus. The disciples suggested Jesus send the crowds away so that they could get food. Jesus called on the disciples to feed them. Andrew brought a small boy with five small barley loaves and two small fish, but Andrew couldn't see how that would be much help for such a large crowd. Jesus instructed his disciples to have the people sit down in the grass. He then took the loaves and fish, gave thanks, and distributed them to the people. The bread and fish multiplied and fed all the people. The left over's filled up twelve baskets. This event was so striking that all four gospel authors tell of this story.[45]

Correcting Misconceptions

The next day the crowd gathered to Jesus and asked him, "What must we do to do the works God requires?" Knowing they were erroneously focused on earning their salvation by works, Jesus responded, "The work of God is this: to believe in the one he has sent." All righteous acts flow from this one single work. Knowing the people were really more concerned with food than righteousness, Jesus described himself as "the bread of life." Jesus said, "He who comes to me will never go hungry, and he who believes in me will never be thirsty. He who believes has everlasting life."[46]

Jesus confronted those who relied on the traditions of men instead of the teachings of God. He quoted the prophet Isaiah in identifying the hypocrites who wore the clothing of a religious leader. As the voice of God, Isaiah proclaimed, "These people honor

---

[44] Mt.8:18, 23-27; Mk.4:35-41; Lk.8:22-25.
[45] Mt.14:15-21; Mk.6:35-44; Lk.9:12-17; Jn.6:4-13.
[46] Jn.6:22-59.

me with their lips, but their hearts are far from me. They worship me in vain; their teachings are but rules taught by men."[47]

Jesus and his disciples came to Caesarea Philippi. Jesus asked, "Who do people say the Son of Man is?" After several suggestions by the disciples, Peter answered, "You are the Christ, the son of the living God." Jesus affirmed Peter's response and said, "I tell you that you are Peter, and on this rock I will build my church and the gates of Hades will not overcome it."[48]

Jesus began explaining to his disciples that he would go to Jerusalem and that he would be killed. Peter refused to accept Jesus' prediction thinking such a thing could never happen to God's messiah. Jesus rebuked Peter and explained that his disciples also needed to have a sacrificial spirit to carry out God's calling. "If anyone would come after me, he must deny himself and take up his cross and follow me."[49]

The Growing Tension with the Religious Leaders

One day while Jesus was teaching in the temple courts the teachers of the law brought a woman caught in adultery and had her stand before Jesus. They reminded Jesus that the Law of Moses required them to stone such a woman and asked him for his response. This was a trap to force Jesus to say something that would get him in trouble. It was against Roman law for the Jews to stone people. Thus the question would force Jesus to side either with the Romans and against the Law of Moses, or with the Law of Moses and against the Romans. Either way, Jesus' answer could be used against him. Instead Jesus responded, "If any one of you is without sin, let him be the first to throw a stone at her." As Jesus' response sank in, they realized the trap had failed. The accusers left one by one, beginning

---

[47]   Mt.15:1-3a, 709; Mk.7:1-23; Jn.7:1.
[48]   Mt.16:13-20; Mk.8:27-30; Lk.9:18-21.
[49]   Mt.16:21-26; Mk.8:31-37; Lk.9:22-25.

with the older ones first. Jesus then turned to the distraught woman and said, "Go now and leave your life of sin."[50]

Lazarus, a good personal friend of Jesus who lived in Bethany, a couple miles outside of Jerusalem, fell into sickness and then death. By the time Jesus arrived Lazarus had been dead and in a tomb for four days. In her sadness Lazarus' sister, Martha, was disappointed that Jesus had not been there to heal her brother. Jesus responded, "I am the resurrection and the life. He who believes in me will live, even though he dies." Jesus asked that the stone be rolled away from the cave that was used as a tomb. After prayer Jesus commanded with a loud voice, "Lazarus come out!" As all watched the cave a man wrapped in burial clothing came out. Lazarus was alive and the people were amazed. Some viewed Jesus as the promised Messiah. Others began plotting the death of Jesus as a dangerous blasphemer.[51]

Almost four years had passed since Jesus began his public ministry with baptism and the calling of his first disciples. It was probably AD 29 or 30, on the Sunday before the Jewish Passover, that Jesus mounted a donkey and rode into Jerusalem with his disciples. This was a well-recognized symbol of kingly authority as Jesus entered by royal procession. The crowds greeted Jesus with palm branches and shouting "Hosanna."[52] The response of the people frightened the religious leaders and they grew more determined to end the life of this prophet.[53]

---

50 Jn.7:53-8:11.
51 *Blasphemer.* Jn.11. "Blasphemy" is a bit like our word "defamation." It is speaking in such a way as "to bring down another's value, honor, due-respect; to injure another's reputation in the eyes of others." *The New Strong's Expanded Dictionary of Bible Words, Ibid*, p.1015, §987. In a religious sense the term was used when someone set himself up in the place of God, thus bringing down God's status to that of mere man. It was an extremely serious offense to the Jews.
52 *Hosanna* comes from the Greek word ωσαννα meaning "save, we pray." *The New Strong's Expanded Dictionary of Bible Words, Ibid*, p.1465, §5614.
53 Mt.21:1-17; Mk.11:1-11; Lk.19:29-44; Jn.12:12-19.

An expert in the law once asked Jesus, "Teacher, which is the greatest commandment in the Law." Jesus summarized the law succinctly in two basic principles, both of which were quotes from the Old Testament.

> "Love the Lord your God with all your heart and with all your soul and with all your mind. This is the first and greatest commandment. And the second is like it: 'Love your neighbor as yourself. All the Law and the Prophets hang on these two commandments."[54]

The Passover Meal

On Thursday evening[55] Jesus met with his apostles in an upper room to celebrate the Passover meal. More than a thousand years earlier, Moses had given the Jews instructions to take a lamb or goat and eat it along with unleavened bread and bitter herbs for the Passover meal.[56] The Passover meal was a reminder of the night the angel of death "passed over" the homes of the Hebrews that had the blood of a slain lamb spread on the doorframe. That night, the first born of the Egyptians, who did not have the blood of a lamb spread on their doorframes, lost their lives. Jesus was about to explain he was the true lamb whose shed blood would save people from spiritual death.

As all were reclining at the low table for the meal, Jesus arose, and put a towel around his waist and poured water into a basin. Performing the task of a servant to get the dirt off the guests' feet

---

[54] Mt.22:34-40; Mk.12:28-34. The commandments Jesus quotes come from Dt.6:5 and Lev.19:18.

[55] *Thursday evening.* This had to be Thursday evening because the next day Jesus was crucified and that day is identified as the day before a special Sabbath. Sabbath began on Friday evening and the Jews did not want bodies hanging on crosses during the Sabbath (Jn.19:31).

[56] Ex.12:5-8.

who would have walked the dusty roads of Jerusalem, Jesus washed the feet of each disciple. Peter protested thinking the master should not wash the feet of the servant. But Jesus explained, "Now that I, your Lord and Teacher, have washed your feet, you also should wash one another's feet. I have set you an example that you should do as I have done for you."[57] The message was clear that all of Jesus' disciples were to be servants.

Moving back to the table Jesus took the unleavened bread, gave thanks, broke it, and gave it to his disciples saying, "Take and eat; this is my body." He then took the cup of wine, gave thanks, offered it to his disciples and said, "Drink from it, all of you. This is my blood of the covenant, which is poured out for many for the forgiveness of sins."[58] This meal has come to be known over the centuries as "the Lord's Supper." Today most churches celebrate a ritualistic form of this meal and call it either "the Lord's Supper," "Communion," or "the Eucharist." It is a time for us to stop and examine ourselves in light of what Jesus has done for us.

Judas, one of the twelve, then left the meal and the upper room. The disciples thought Judas was probably going to get some more food for the meal. In reality, he was making his way to the Jewish leaders with whom he had agreed to betray Jesus for the payment of 30 pieces of silver.[59]

Jesus explained that he would be leaving to prepare a place for his disciples. He told them they knew the way to the place where he was going. Thomas did not understand and asked how they could know the way. Jesus responded, "I am the way the truth and the life. No one comes to the Father except through me." Philip then asked Jesus to show them God the Father. Jesus turned to Philip and said, "Anyone who has seen me has seen the Father."[60]

---

[57] Jn.13:1-20.
[58] Mt.26:26-29; Mk.14:22-25; Lk.22:17-20; 1Co.11:23-26.
[59] Mt.26:21-25; Mk.14:18-21; Lk.22:21-23; Jn.13:21-30.
[60] Jn.14:1-14.

Following supper, Jesus and the Apostles walked across the Kidron Valley to a garden known as Gethsemane, just outside of the city of Jerusalem at the Mount of Olives. Jesus went off to pray while his apostles rested. Knowing what was to come, Jesus fell to his knees in prayer. After some time in agonizing prayer Jesus pleaded, "My Father, if it is possible, may this cup be taken from me. Yet not as I will, but as you will." Jesus returned to the Apostles who had fallen asleep and woke them just as Judas was leading the Jewish guards into the garden. Judas identified Jesus in the night with a kiss and the guards seized Jesus.[61]

The Trial of Jesus

Jesus was first brought before Annas, the father-in-law to Caiaphas, the Jewish high priest that year. In response to the interrogation Jesus explained, "I always taught in synagogues or at the temple, where all the Jews come together. I said nothing in secret." One of the officials suddenly struck Jesus in the face. Jesus was then taken to the high priest where many were assembled for a mockery of a trial. After interviewing many witness who gave the leaders no facts upon which to build a case against Jesus, two came forward declaring Jesus had said he would destroy the temple and rebuild it in three days. Jesus remained silent as they asked him questions until they demanded, "Tell us if you are the Christ, the Son of God?" Jesus said, "Yes, it is as you say." The high priest tore his clothes, as was the custom when a pious Jew was appalled at sinful behavior, and the crowd responded that Jesus was worthy of death for placing himself in the place of God. They spit in his face, struck him with their fists, slapped him and taunted him with "Prophesy to us, Christ. Who hit you?"[62]

---

[61] Mt.26:30-56; Mk.14:26-52; Lk.22:39-53; Jn.18:1-12.
[62] Mt.26:57-68; Mk.14:53-65; Lk.22:54a.

Peter had made his way into the courtyard of the structure where the trial was occurring to get as close as he could to his Lord. Three times people in the courtyard recognized Peter as a disciple and confronted him with this fact. Three times Peter denied that he even knew Jesus. The third time, two things happened that hit Peter with such force that he was left devastated. First a rooster crowed signaling the break of day. Earlier that evening, while Peter was boldly proclaiming his loyalty, Jesus had warned that Peter would deny Jesus three times before the rooster crowed. Secondly, just as the rooster was crowing, Jesus, beaten and tired, looked at Peter and their eyes met. Peter ran from this place and wept bitterly. This "rock" had crumbled.[63]

Jesus was taken to Pilate, the Roman governor, because the Jews did not have legal authority to execute Jesus. Pilate asked, "Are you the king of the Jews?" Jesus replied, "Yes, it is as you say." Jesus continued,

> My kingdom is not of this world. If it were, my servants would fight to prevent my arrest by the Jews. ... You are right in saying I am a king. In fact, for this reason I was born, and for this I came into the world, to testify to the truth. Everyone on the side of truth listens to me.[64]

Frustrated and hopeless Pilate vented, "What is truth?" Pilate went out to the Jews and explained he couldn't find any basis for a charge against Jesus.[65]

In hopes that he could induce the Jews to let him release Jesus, Pilate explained that there was a custom at Passover time by which Pilate could release a prisoner. So he asked, whether they wanted him to release Jesus, or the murdering rebel, Barabbas. In an orchestrated response the crowd demanded the release of

---

[63] Mt.26:58-75; Mk.14:54-72; Lk.22:54-62; Jn.18:15-18.
[64] Jn.18:36-37.
[65] Mt.27:2-14; Mk.15:1-5; Lk.23:1-5; Jn.18:28-38.

Barabbas and the crucifixion of Jesus. Again hoping to dissuade the Jews, Pilate had Jesus flogged. Floggings were so severe that many did not survive them. [66] The soldiers put a crown made of long sharp Judean thorns on the head of Jesus and Pilate brought the exhausted bloody Jesus out to the people. The crowd continued to call for crucifixion. Pilate asked why, but the crowd persisted. Pilate gave up, washed his hands in a symbolic ritual, and ordered the crucifixion.[67]

The Crucifixion and Death of Jesus

Crucifixion was a cruel deterrent to lawlessness, by which a non-Roman citizen would be stripped of his clothing, tied or nailed to a wooden cross, and left to die. Jesus was made to carry his own cross, or at least the cross bar of the cross, to Golgotha, a hill upon which Jesus and two other criminals would be crucified. Part way towards Golgotha, the soldiers picked Simon the Cyrene from the crowd and made him carry Jesus' cross, probably because Jesus was too beaten and weak to carry the heavy wooden instrument of his own execution. A large number of people followed, mourned and wailed for Jesus.[68]

It was about 9 in the morning when the soldiers stripped Jesus of his clothing and nailed him to a cross between the two other criminals.[69] The soldiers attached a sign to the cross above the head of Jesus that read in Hebrew, Greek and Latin, "JESUS OF NAZARETH, THE KING OF THE JEWS." Some of the people mocked Jesus as he hung on the cross. Bloody, beaten, and hanging from the

---

[66] Josephus, Wars, Book 2, 21:5, cited in the *Life of Jesus Christ*, online at http://www.jesus-story.net/scourging.htm.

[67] Mt.27:15-26; Mk.15:6-15; Lk.23:13-25; Jn.18:39-19:16.

[68] Mt.27:31-34; Mk.15:20-23; Lk.23:26-33; Jn.19:16-17.

[69] *Stripped of his clothing.* It is a bit unclear as to whether Jesus was able to keep his undergarment or not when stripped of his clothing and nailed to the cross.

cross, Jesus looked down on the Jews and Romans and sadly asked, "Father, forgive them, for they do not know what they are doing." One of the crucified criminals also mocked Jesus. The criminal on the other side of Jesus rebuked the first one and pleaded, "Jesus, remember me when you come into your kingdom." Jesus struggled to answer, "I tell you the truth, today you will be with me in paradise." The Apostle John, and several women, including Jesus' mother, were at the foot of the cross.[70]

It grew dark from noon to 3 pm. At about 3 pm Jesus cried out in Aramaic, *"Eloi, Eloi, lama sabachthani"* which meant, "My God, my God, why have you forsaken me?" Shortly thereafter Jesus said with his last dying breath, "It is finished. Father, into your hands I commit my spirit." Then, on that dark Friday afternoon, he bowed his head and died.[71]

The curtain across the entrance to the Holy of Holies in the Temple was made of one heavy single piece of material.[72] To enter the back room of the Temple known as the Holy of Holies, one would have to enter from the outside edge of the curtain to go in. At the moment of Jesus' death, that curtain tore in two from top to bottom. The earth shook and rocks split. There were even stories of dead people rising to life. It seems the world had been shaken at its very foundations. The Roman centurion watching the crucifixion was terrified and said, "Surely he was the Son of God."[73]

Jesus' side was pierced with a spear to confirm his death. Joseph of Arimathea was granted permission to take the body of Jesus down and bury him. Jesus was wrapped in linen cloth and placed in

---

[70] Mt.27:35-44; Mk.15:24-32; Lk.23:33-43; Jn.19:18-27.

[71] Mt.27:45-50; Mk.15:33-37; Lk.23:44-46; Jn.19:28-30.

[72] *Temple curtain.* The Old Testament provides considerable detail on all the curtains and veils used in the Tabernacle and Temple. A veil of blue, purple, crimson and fine linen hung between the Holy Place and the Holy of Holies in the Tabernacle and then the Temple (Ex.26:31-33; 2Chr.3:14). The Bible describes a single veil or curtain between the Holy Place and the Holy of Holies.

[73] Mt.27:51-56; Mk.15:38-41; Lk.23:45-49.

a tomb cut out of rock. A large stone was rolled against the entrance to the tomb. It was Friday evening.[74]

The Priests asked Pilate to place a guard at the tomb because there had been a rumor that Jesus would be raised from the dead. They warned the governor that there could be trouble if the disciples stole Jesus' body away and then claimed he was resurrected. So Pilate gave orders to seal the tomb and posted guards.[75]

The Resurrection of Jesus

Friday evening, and all day Saturday, the disciples were in shock and huddling in the upper room. On Sunday morning, the third day, there was another earthquake. An angel rolled back the stone of the tomb and sat on it. The guards were terrified and fled. Mary Magdalene, Mary the mother of James, and Salome went to the tomb carrying spices to anoint the body of Jesus. When they arrived at the tomb they found no guards, the stone rolled away, the body of Jesus missing, and two angels who said, "Why do you look for the living among the dead? He is not here; he has risen!" The women hurried from the tomb feeling a mixture of fear, confusion and joy.[76]

The women returned to the upper room and told the eleven remaining apostles what they had seen, but the apostles didn't believe them. Peter however, did get up and started running for the tomb. John also ran for the tomb, and because he was faster than Peter, arrived first. John stood outside the tomb and waited as Peter rushed inside to find the linen cloths, but no body. Bewildered they left the tomb.[77]

There were growing reports from people who claimed to have seen Jesus alive. Then while most of the apostles were gathered together in one room, Jesus appeared among them saying, "Peace be

---

[74] Mt.27:59-60; Mk.15:46; Lk.23:54; Jn.19:39-42.
[75] Lk.23:55-56.
[76] Mt.28:5-8; Mk.16:2-8; Lk.24:1-8; Lk.24:1-8.
[77] Lk.24:9-12; Jn.20:2-10.

with you." Thomas was not present and when told of the appearance he was skeptical and responded, "Unless I see the nail marks in his hands and put my finger where the nails were, and put my hand into his side, I will not believe it." A week later, they were gathered again in the house and this time Thomas was with them. Jesus appeared again and said to Thomas, "Put your finger here; see my hands. Reach out your hand and put it into my side. Stop doubting and believe." Thomas proclaimed, "My Lord and my God!"[78]

The eleven apostles met Jesus again at a mountain in Galilee where they worshipped him. Jesus commissioned them for the great work ahead, saying,

> "All authority in heaven and on earth has been given to me. Therefore go and make disciples of all nations, baptizing them in the name of the Father and of the Son and of the Holy Spirit, and teaching them to obey everything I have commanded you. And surely I am with you always, to the very end of the age."[79]

The last time Jesus met with the disciples was in the vicinity of Bethany, one of Jesus' favorite places. Jesus blessed the disciples and was taken up before their eyes towards heaven until a cloud hid him from their view. Two angels then appeared and asked, "Why do you stand here looking into the sky? This same Jesus, who has been taken from you into heaven, will come back in the same way you have seen him go into heaven." The disciples left and returned to Jerusalem – to wait.[80]

---

[78] Mk.16:14; Lk.24:36-43; Jn.20:19-31.
[79] Mt.28:16-20; Mk.16:15-18.
[80] Mk.16:19-20; Lk.24:50-53; Ac.1:9-12.

Summary

Born of a virgin, impregnated by the Holy Spirit, announced by angels, and worshipped by wise men, God broke into the world in human form. As a man, he taught with knowledge and conviction. He preached the importance of attitudes, and not just actions. He turned people's attention to God for guidance in life. He challenged the religious leaders. He healed the sick, gave sight to the blind, enabled lame men to walk, and even gave life to the dead. The Jewish leaders trumped up a charge, enlisted the Romans to help, and crucified the Son of God. Jesus was buried in a tomb, closed with a large stone and sealed by the Romans. But that was Friday afternoon. By Sunday morning, the stone was rolled away, the tomb was empty, and Jesus had been resurrected to life.

Thought Questions

1. In what ways did Jesus stand out from humanity at large?

2. At what point in the ministry of Jesus do you think the disciples came to believe Jesus was the Messiah and savior?

3. What impact has the story of Jesus had on society over the past 2,000 years?

4. Why do you think the story has had such an impact?

5. What most impresses you about this story?

2

For

For...

Why Did They Care?

Sometimes an understanding of the motivation behind an action is the key to understanding the action itself. I learned something about this principle years ago. I was initially confused about the church because I couldn't fathom what energized its members. It took more than a cursory association with the church to comprehend its driving force.

Prior to college, living on the Maryland side of Washington, DC, I had limited involvement with church. My grandmother on my dad's side had been very active with her church. She gave me my first Bible when I was very young. Dad had then taken my brothers and me to church every Easter for several years. There were occasional times when I might attend with Dad for a series of consecutive weeks, but that never lasted. Perhaps that was because Dad traveled a lot. Or perhaps I just lost interest. Whatever the reason, I never really got plugged into a church, got to know the people outside of Sunday morning's service, or to form any relationship with God.

I left the Washington DC area for college in Montana. Upon starting college in Bozeman, Montana, I met a fellow freshman who introduced me to a local church on Church Night[1] during Orientation Week that welcomed me and invited me in. I initially started attending because I had met a young woman that first night I thought I might like to date, but that quickly passed and I kept attending. Perhaps something I saw in my grandmother or my irregular visits to church back east as a child had sparked my interest in Christ. In Montana, I kept going back. I grew to know people from multiple Christian families from that church. I became involved in adult Bible study. I ate meals at member's homes. I got involved in ministry activities with other members. I met with members in all kinds of different situations and found people who genuinely seemed to care about people. The church there took me in even before I made my decision for Christ.

I saw God's love both in the Bible and in the families of that church who committed themselves to reach out to those who had needs. I experienced it in the way they reached out and cared for me as a college student in a place far away from home. I witnessed their dedication to the church and its mission to reach out and help not only its own members, but those in the surrounding community. The building was nothing special. The church only had about 150 members. The music wasn't anything that would impress outsiders. There was nobody at the church who had any extraordinary wealth, power, or stardom. What I saw fascinated me. Why would these people give so much to this little church and its surrounding community?

In April of my freshman year, after being associated with these Christians for about eight months, I called the minister of that church to discuss my fascination and confusion. *Why* were they so committed and so ready to reach out to those who were struggling - even to new people like me? *Why* did they love and care

---

[1] *Church Night.* I don't know the official MSU name for this event. I'm sure it was also for Jews to plug into a local synagogue and others to plug in to their local religious groups.

so much? The minister came to the student center and we talked for a couple hours. I explained that I wasn't sure I believed everything in the Bible and didn't understand how the members could give so much time to this Christian effort. Yet I had seen the love and hope of God displayed in the lives of the church members. They were committed to something or someone bigger than themselves. I wanted what they had. The minister told me I didn't need to understand everything. I only needed to commit to let God lead and show me the way. God would teach and reveal what I needed to know as I walked with him over time. I agreed that I could do that. That week I was baptized and committed my life to God through Jesus.[2] My understanding of the power that fueled this dynamic Christian living would build over decades as I came to know God and God's people.

The Biblical Context

The Apostle John begins chapter 3 verse 16 of his Gospel (aka John 3:16) with a Greek phrase, ουτως γαρ, most commonly translated "for." John uses this word (2 words in the Greek) to introduce us to the heart of the Gospel. He is about to concisely tell us *what* God has done for mankind and *why* in terms so simple and powerful that they have moved millions of people for thousands of years. I asked the question "Why?" when I was introduced to the Montana church. The Apostle John answered my question in this poignant verse and he introduced the verse with "for."

---

[2] *Baptism* is a ritual representing (1) a decision made for Christ – Ac.2:37-39, (2) a uniting with Christ in his death, burial and resurrection – Ro.6:3-7, (3) a putting on of Christ – Gal.3:27, and (4) an appeal to God for a clear conscience – 1 Pe.3:20-21. The English word, "baptism," is a *transliteration* of the Greek term, βαπτισμα (baptisma), meaning "immersion, submersion and emergence" (*The New Strong's Expanded Dictionary of Bible Words*, James Strong, Nashville, TN: Thomas Nelson Publishers, 2001, §908, p.1006.

It is always good to examine a statement within its context. The context typically gives the statement more depth and power. For instance, the Gettysburg Address would lose much of its power if it were separated from its setting in the Civil War. Additionally it is very easy to misunderstand a statement if it is completely lifted from its context. Politicians fear the day when they say something that a news reporter will publish without explaining its context. To ensure we get the context right on John 3:16, we will begin with an overview of the construction of the Bible itself and then move to a focus on the immediate context of our verse.

The Bible includes two different "testaments" that came at different points of time for God's people. The Old Testament is made up of 39 documents, written primarily in Hebrew, containing the laws and principles by which the Jews lived.[3] The final 27 documents of the Bible are known collectively as the New Testament and focus on Jesus Christ, the Son of God. These New Testament documents were originally written in Greek in the 1st century AD and form the basis for Christian life. These 66 books were the result of many human authors inspired by God's special revelation.[4] Both testaments tell of God's love, the consequences of sin, and the need for devotion to God.

As an attorney, trained in estate-planning legal principles, I think of a "Testament" as an estate-planning document (Trust or Will). It is a statement of desire by the Testator (Testament maker) of what he expects of his people, and the inheritance to which they are entitled as beneficiaries. It is probably more like a trust in that both the Old Testament and New Testament provide guidance during the life of the committed follower much like a trust does during the life of the beneficiary. God is the Testator or Settlor.

---

[3]   Although the Hebrew Bible has fewer than 39 books, it contains the same material as our modern English Bibles. Our English Bibles simply divide up the material in a different way.

[4]   2Pe.1:20-21.

There are even a series of provisions in the Old Testament and New Testament that resemble the type of no-contest clauses we sometimes see in Wills and Trusts today. They provide that one will not receive his or her promised inheritance if the individual contests God's plan or declines to live in God's family.

The twenty-seven documents that make up the New Testament are written by men who either walked with and personally interacted with Jesus, or who sat at the feet of those who did and learned about Jesus first hand from eyewitnesses.[5] These are the writers who had immediate authority to teach about Jesus. Their writings were generally accepted, when written, as having the same level of authority as the Old Testament Scriptures.[6] Centuries later, church leaders met and decided on a formal list of New Testament Scripture, primarily to exclude other documents propagated by heretics. This list was called "the Canon."

> The English word *canon* goes back to the Greek word *kanon* and then to the Hebrew *qaneh*. Its basic meaning is *reed*, our English word *cane* being derived from it. Since a reed was sometimes used as a measuring rod, the word *kanon* came to mean a standard or rule. It was also used to refer to a list or index, and when applied to the Bible denotes the list of books which are received as Holy Scripture.[7]

---

[5] *Eyewitness.* The Apostle Paul was an eyewitness of Jesus by means of vision (Ac.9:1-19; 22:6-11; 1Co.15:8). Within this vision he interacted with Jesus personally and was called to be an apostle like the Twelve.

[6] *Immediate Scriptural authority.* 2Pe.3:15-16; 2nd Clement, written at the end of the 1st century, references Isaiah 54:1 and then writes, "and the author goes on: 'And another Scripture says 'I came not to call the righteous, but sinner," a direct quote from Mt.9:13). *The Canon of Scripture*, by F. F. Bruce, Downers Grove, IL: Intervarsity Press, 1988, p.121.

[7] *How We Got the Bible*, by Neil R. Lightfoot, Grand Rapids, MI: Baker Book House 1963, p.81.

"Canon," in regards to the New Testament, refers to the collection of documents leaders in the church eventually determined to have been written by eyewitnesses to Jesus, or those who learned the story from eyewitnesses. There were various informal lists of New Testament books in the first several centuries of the church. There was even some uncertainty in the fourth century about the authors of a few of the manuscripts proposed for inclusion in the formal Canon, like Hebrews and 2nd Peter. In these cases, it was determined that although there was some uncertainty about the authorship, the writings were consistent with the other documents accepted as Scripture and they had the nature and feel of one who knew Jesus or learned of Jesus from an eyewitness. They also had a tradition of having been accepted as Scripture by the early church.

The first four documents of the New Testament, known as "books," are called "gospels." Our English term "gospel" comes from a Greek term ευαγγελιον (*euaggelion*) meaning "a good message"[8] or "good news."[9] The story of the life and ministry of Jesus is called the "gospel" or "good news" because it brings eternal hope to all who will listen and follow. It is called the greatest love story of all time because it reveals the depth of God's love and the ends to which God will go to bring people into His family.

The Gospel of John is the fourth gospel in the New Testament and was written towards the end of the 1st century AD by a man

---

[8] *The New Strong's Expanded Dictionary of Bible Words*, by James Strong, Nashville: Thomas Nelson Publishers, 2001, §2098, p.1116.

[9] *Shorter Lexicon of the Greek New Testament*, by F. Wilbur Gingrich, Chicago: The University of Chicago Press, 1965, ευαγγελιον, p.85.

named John.[10] He was one of the earliest disciples of Christ.[11] John was the son of Zebedee who was a fisherman wealthy enough to hire servants.[12] His mother was Salome.[13] John was the brother

---

[10] *Author of the Gospel of John.* Even though the Gospel of John identifies its author as simply "the disciple whom Jesus loved" (Jn.21:20-24) and not by name, there are a number of reasons to conclude John the Apostle was that disciple and the writer of this Gospel. (1) There were "the twelve" (a designation for the 12 Apostles) at the last supper with Jesus (Mt.26:20; Mk.14:17). "The disciple whom Jesus loved" was reclining next to Jesus at that supper and thus one of the 12 apostles (Jn.13:23). (2) The Apostle John was one of the inner circle of Jesus (Peter, James & John in Mk.5:37; Mt.17:1; Mt.26:37; Mk.14:33) which would be consistent with the label "the disciple whom Jesus loved." The writer of the Gospel of John and letters attributed to John emphasize the author's connection to Jesus. The writer knew Jesus well. (3) Additionally several ancient writers identified the Apostle John as the "disciple whom Jesus loved", the disciple who reclined next to Jesus at the last supper, and the disciple who wrote the Gospel of John. Polycarp (who was mentored by the Apostle John) wrote "John, who was both a witness and a teacher, who reclined upon the bosom of the Lord, ..." (Eusebius, H.E. 3.31.3). Irenaeus, bishop of Lyons (who was mentored by Polycarp) wrote, "John, the disciple of the Lord, who leaned on his breast, also published the gospel while living at Ephesus in Asia" (Adv Haer.3.1.2). Clement of Alexandria wrote, "Last of all John, perceiving that the bodily facts had been made plain in the gospel, being urged by his friends, and inspired by the Spirit, composed a spiritual gospel" (Eusebius, H.E. 4.14.7). He also claimed John went to Ephesus after Domitian's death. The Muratorian Canon (AD 180-200) included the following explanation, "The fourth gospel is by John, one of the disciples. When his fellow-disciples and bishops exhorted him he said, 'Today fast with me for three days, ...'" The Anti Muratorian prologue to Luke states, "According to Papias, the dear disciple of John, in his five exegetical books, this gospel was published and sent to the churches of Asia by John himself during his lifetime." See *Word Biblical Commentary*, *John*, Vol.36, by George R. Beasley-Murray, Nashville, TN: Thomas Nelson Publishers, 1999, pp.lxvi-lxxv.

[11] Mt.4:18-22.

[12] Mk.1:19-20.

[13] *John's mother.* Compare Mt.27:55-56 which mentions the "mother of Zebedee's sons" as present with Mary Magdalene, and Mary the mother of James and Joses at the cross, with Mk.15:40 which mentions Mary Magdalene, Mary mother of James the younger and Joses, and Salome

of James.[14] Both James and John were Galilean fishermen. They were called "sons of thunder," indicating a fiery temperament or religious zeal.[15] This is quite extraordinary in light of the emphasis John places on "love" in his writings. Clearly Jesus had a dramatic effect on John's heart. Both John and James would have known Peter before meeting Jesus, as they were fishing partners with Simon Peter.[16]

John was one of the Twelve Apostles.[17] The term "apostle" referred to a "messenger" or "one who has been sent."[18] For us it is easier to think of this person as an "ambassador of the Gospel" or a "commissioner of Christ." The term "apostle" is often used in a special narrow sense in relation to Christ as one who interacted with Jesus face to face and was commissioned personally by Jesus to spread the Good News. It is also used in a broader sense of one who accepted the calling of God to spread the Good News, without

---

at the cross. Clearly the same three women are being described. Thus "Salome" of Mk.15 must be "the mother of Zebedee's sons" mentioned in Mt.27. 16:1 identifies the same three women again (Mary Magdalene, Mary mother of James and Salome) as bringing spices to anoint the body of Jesus.

[14] Mt.4:18-22; 10:1-6.

[15] *Sons of Thunder.* James and John exhibited some temperamental zeal during the life of Jesus (Lk.9:49-50; Lk.9:52-56; Mk.10:35-37). There are also stories of John's excitable temperament in his old age. "In *Against Heresies*, Irenaeus relates how Polycarp told a story of 'the disciple of the Lord, going to bathe at Ephesus, and perceiving Cerinthus within, rushed out of the bath-house without bathing, exclaiming, "Let us fly, lest even the bath-house fall down, because Cerinthus, the enemy of the truth, is within." *John the Apostle,* online at http://en.wikipedia.org/wiki/ John_the_Apostle.

[16] Lk.5:10.

[17] Mt.10:1-6.

[18] *Apostle* (αποστολος) *The New Strong's Expanded Dictionary of Bible Words,* by James Strong, Nashville, TN: Thomas Nelson Publishers, 2001, §652, p.982.

having seen Jesus face to face.[19] The term "Apostle," with a capital "A," is frequently used to refer to those who were personally called by Jesus during his life on earth.

John was one of the three in the inner circle of Jesus' closest Apostles.[20] He was the disciple whom the Lord loved"[21] which evidences a close relationship and may indicate John was taken in by Jesus as a type of younger brother, or son.[22] John personally saw the empty tomb and the risen Christ.[23]

John does not stand out as a leader of the early church during the period covered by the Book of Acts (up to perhaps AD 62 or thereabouts). His brother, James, on the other hand was the first Apostle martyred for his faith.[24] Over time, as the other Apostles died off one by one, and as John matured and moved in to his old age, he increased in prominence.

John probably wrote his Gospel somewhere between AD 85-95 when he was an elderly man.[25] The book reflects a deep contemplation of the meaning of the events described. It has long been held that the other three Gospels (Matthew, Mark and Luke) had already been completed and widely circulated. John's Gospel

---

[19] *Apostles who did not meet Jesus in person.* Barnabas (Ac.14:4, 14), Andronicus and Junias (Ro.16:7), 2 unnamed brethren (2 Co.8:23), Epaphroditus (Php.2:25), & Silas and Timothy (1Th.2:6) are each called αποστολος. There is no evidence to indicate any of these personally met Jesus face to face.

[20] Mk.5:37; Mt.17:1; Mt.26:37/Mk.14:33.

[21] Jn.13:23; 19:26; 20:2; 21:7; 21:20.

[22] Jn.19:26-27. May be a bit like Joseph caring for his younger brother, Benjamin in Genesis 42-43. John is generally considered to be the youngest of the 12 Apostles.

[23] Jn.20:4-19.

[24] Ac.12:2.

[25] *Earliest copy.* The earliest copy of the Gospel of John that exists today is in a collection of some fragments dated the first half of the 2nd century AD. The John Ryland Fragments are being kept at the John Rylands University Library, Manchester, England. *The Text of the New Testament*, by Bruce Metzger, New York & Oxford: Oxford University Press, 1968, pp.38-39.

was completely fresh. Although many of its accounts overlap with the other three Gospels, John focuses on that which was *not* covered in the prior three Gospels, explaining at the end that it would be impossible to write about everything that Jesus did because so many volumes would be needed to cover the story.[26]

The Immediate Context for Our Verse

The subject of our study is John 3:16. This single verse is the summary and conclusion of a prior discussion between Jesus and a man named Nicodemus.

The story begins in John 3:1 with Nicodemus, who was a Pharisee, and member of the Jewish Sanhedrin, coming to Jesus secretly by night early in Jesus' public ministry to learn more about this unusual preacher. The Pharisees were a conservative group of blue-collar type workers who believed the entire Old Testament was the Word of God. They took the Old Testament seriously and studied it meticulously to understand what God wanted from his people.[27] The Sanhedrin was the local ruling council that had authority over the Jews and the Jewish Temple.[28] The Sanhedrin was made up *primarily* of Sadducees, who were wealthier and better connected Jews than the Pharisees. Sadducees believed only the first five books of the Bible were divinely inspired. The rest of the Old Testament was treated as inspirational and encouragement, but not as *divine revelation*.[29] It's somewhat like the way we treat contemporary Christian authors today. We distinguish between the Bible, as the Word of God by divine revelation, and modern Christian writers, as gifted but not inspired through special divine

---

[26] Jn.20:30-31.

[27] *The International Standard Bible Encyclopaedia*, Grand Rapids, MI: Wm B. Eerdmans Publishing Co., 1956, Vol.IV, "Pharisees," p.2361.

[28] *Ibid*, "Sanhedrin," pp.2688-2690.

[29] *Ibid*, Sadducees," pp.2658-2661.

revelation. The majority of the Sanhedrin took a dim view of Jesus' radical ideas. Thus Nicodemus, a member of this austere council, went to Jesus at night to conceal his interest.[30]

Nicodemus started the conversation by acknowledging that God had sent Jesus. After all, no one could reasonably deny the power of the miracles done by Jesus. It's as if Nicodemus was trying to get the conversation going, but wasn't quite sure how to direct it where he wanted it to go.

Jesus abruptly brought the conversation to the very core of the question Nicodemus was trying to ask and provided an answer. "I tell you the truth, no one can see the kingdom of God unless he is born again."[31] Nicodemus was confused, thinking, "How can one be born *physically* a second time?" Jesus repeated his point, "I tell you the truth, no one can enter the kingdom of God unless he is born of water and the Spirit."[32] Jesus clarified that one must be born again *spiritually.* Jesus continued to describe how the Spirit is unseen and how difficult it is to describe spiritual things to people who perceive the world physically.

This "kingdom" referenced by Jesus in this conversation, was not a physical kingdom with lands and boundaries. The Jews had hoped that a messiah (anointed savior) would come, reign as a king on earth, and serve much like the revered King David had served

---

[30] *Conceal his interest.* Nicodemus stood up for Jesus without revealing he was a disciple (Jn.7:45-52). Following the death of Jesus, Nicodemus joined up with Joseph of Arimathea, who was a "secret disciple" for fear of the Jews, to take the body of Jesus down from the cross and bury it in a garden tomb (Jn.19:38-42).

[31] Jn.3:3. *Water and the Spirit.* For the first 1800 years of Christianity, John 3:5 ("water and spirit") was almost always thought to refer to one event - baptism (Acts 2:38 ties baptism and the Spirit together). In the ancient church "baptism" was synonymous with "new birth" and "conversion." In this sense John may have been recording an event focusing on conversion, which, in ancient times, *always* involved baptism. Others view "water" as referring to a natural birth and "the Spirit" referring to the spiritual birth.

[32] Jn.3:5.

during his life around the turn of the century in 1,000 BC. But Jesus taught the kingdom was not a physical place.

> [20]Once, having been asked by the Pharisees when the kingdom of God would come, Jesus replied, "The kingdom of God does not come with your careful observation, [21]nor will people say, 'Here it is,' or 'There it is,' because the kingdom of God is within you."[33]

The "kingdom" has to do with relationships, not physical places. It is the relationship between king and subject. The form of this Kingdom comes in phases (the Old Testament Kingdom of Israel, the period of the Church, the eternal heavenly Kingdom, etc.).[34] This is why the Kingdom could be viewed as present and also as still coming in the future. A future phase always existed. The Kingdom's central feature is always the relationship between King and subjects, and not territory or places. Wherever and whenever God, or God through Jesus, is respected as King by his subjects - there the Kingdom exists.[35] We might call these subjects, "Kingdom People."

Jesus, or the author of the Gospel, or perhaps God, the Author behind the author, then brought us verse 16 - the verse that ties it all together. This is the verse that explains with amazing brevity, what it means to be born again, born spiritually, and to enter the kingdom of God. This verse describes how the new birth is even possible and why God offers us the chance to be adopted as a part of his family.

---

[33] Lk.17:20-21.

[34] *Kingdom passages.* Ps.103:19; 145:1, 11; Ex.15:18; 19:5-6; Jdge.8:22-23; 17:6; 18:1; 19:1; 21:25; Mt.3:1-2; 4:17; 6:9-10; 6:33; 12:28; Mk.10:15; Jn.18:36.

[35] *The New Strong's Expanded Dictionary of Bible Words*, by James Strong, Nashville, TN: Thomas Nelson Publishers, 2001, §4427 מֶלֶךְ, p.610.

For

"For" indicates purpose or cause. We can see this in other types of similar sentences. *"For* he was so confident in his ability that he took on the challenging assignment." *"For* he was so hungry that he ate the cold mush put in front of him." *"For* she loved him so much that she agreed to marry him." The term "for" alerts us that the reason for an action is about to be presented.[36]

Thus one of the factors that makes John 3:16 a favorite in the Bible is that this passage gives us the *reason* for the difficult ministry and crucifixion of Jesus. We see clearly *why* God is acting. We know his motivation. Without this motivation on God's part, the events described in the passage would not make any sense. They would be too fantastic. There has to be a strong and powerful motivation and purpose for God to implement such a drastic and difficult plan of action. When we understand the motivation, we gain a much better understanding of the plan, the action and the resulting events. When we understand the motivation, we appreciate what has and is being done by God for each of us.

Summary

Christ's coming to earth was an amazing action and there was an even more amazing motivation behind the action. The reason itself is so powerful that people throughout the world and history have been struck, moved and broken by its depth. If you truly understand

---

[36] In regards to the Greek, the term "γαρ" is a "conjunction used to express cause." (Shorter Lexicon of the Greek New Testament, by F. Wilbur Gingrich, Chicago: The University of Chicago Press, 1965, γαρ, p.40.) It is most commonly translated "for." It is coupled here with the Greek term "ουτως" which means "in this manner, thus, so." (Ibid, ουτως, p.156.) Together they could be translated "for thus." (The NIV Interlinear Greek-English New Testament, by Alfred Marshall, Grand Rapids, Mich: Zondervan Corp., p.366.)

the reason behind Christ's coming – really understand – you cannot walk away from this passage and God's action without a deep sense of conviction, graditude, and commitment.

Thought Questions

1. What strikes you about the way the Bible is put together and organized?

2. What differences or similarities are there between the Old Testament and the New Testament?

3. Why do you think there are four gospels, instead of just one?

4. What is special about John's gospel?

5. Why would Nicodemus, a leader of the Jews, be fearful to be seen talking with Jesus?

6. What do you think of when you hear the phrase "Kingdom of God?"

3

God

For God...

"God" is the central character of the Bible - the best selling book in history.[1] Between 80-90% of the world's population believe in god in some form.[2] About 1/3 of the world's population count themselves "Christian."[3] The Bible identifies and describes the one true God for all mankind.

---

[1] *Bible as best selling book.* "The Bible is widely considered to be the best selling book of all time, has estimated annual sales of 100 million copies, and has been a major influence on literature and history, especially in the West where it was the first mass-printed book. The Gutenberg Bible was the first Bible ever printed using movable type." *Bible* online at http://en.wikipedia.org/wiki/Bible.

[2] (1) "The study detailed Americans' deep and broad religiosity, finding that 92 percent believe in God or a universal spirit -- including one in five of those who call themselves atheists. More than half of Americans polled pray at least once a day." [The Washington Post, *Jacqueline L. Salmon,* Washington Post Staff Writer, Tuesday, June 24, 2008; Page A02.] (2) A 12/15/09 Harris Poll found that "the great majority (82%) of American adults believe in God, exactly the same number as in two earlier Harris Polls in 2005 and 2007. Large majorities also believe in miracles (76%), heaven (75%), that Jesus is God or the Son of God (73%), in angels (72%), the survival of the soul after death (71%), and in the resurrection of Jesus (70%)." [http://www.harrisinteractive.com/vault/Harris_Poll_2009_12_15.pdf]

[3] Christians 33.32% (of which Roman Catholics 16.99%, Protestants 5.78%, Orthodox 3.53%, Anglicans 1.25%), Muslims 21.01%, Hindus 13.26%, Buddhists 5.84%, Sikhs 0.35%, Jews 0.23%, Baha'is 0.12%,

Defining "God"

Definitions for "god" can vary. However, they tend to focus on a being or object with extraordinary power that is worshipped by people. There are two elements of this definition. A "god" is typically ascribed some type of supernatural power, above and beyond what we ordinary mortals can exercise. A "god" also has priority in one's life. A being or thing with these qualities tends to be treated with worship and awe. Worship can be "worship" even if the term is not used.

The Bible speaks of many "false gods" or "idols." Some were statues of wood or stone carved to look like earthly creatures.[4] Some were simply imaginary beings devised in the minds of people as supernatural. The Bible even identifies attitudes like evil desires and greed as false gods or idols.[5] They are "gods" because of the priority some people give to them. These are "false" because the only power they really have is the power the believer gives to them in his or her own life.[6]

Even in today's modern age, false gods are prevalent. Many still hold strong superstitious beliefs. Violation of those superstitions causes anxiety in the believer. Some focus exorbitantly on the evil forces of the world, thus giving those forces power in that person's life. We also have a tendency to worship extraordinary people like politicians, musicians, actors, and athletes because they have the power to do that which we cannot. We may worship the human body as if achieving a strong and beautiful body will result in all one wants in life. Money and financial success often become false gods. This grows out of the erroneous belief that money can provide all that we need.

---

other religions 11.78%, non-religious 11.77%, atheists 2.32% (2007 est.) *[https://en.wikipedia.org/wiki/List_of_religious_populations]*.

[4]   Dt.4:28; Isa.40:20; Jer.10:5; Ac.17:29.
[5]   Col.3:5.
[6]   Dt.4:28; Isa.45:20.

The Bible also describes a different type of god - a supreme being of the spiritual dimension, not limited by the laws of physics. This god exists independently of anything we believe and any priorities we set. This god is not a human invention. He does not get his power from our belief. Rather our belief comes from his powerful existence. We identify this "god" as *the* "God" with a capital "G."

This God identified himself to Moses more than three thousand years ago. While shepherding in the Sinai desert Moses caught sight of a strange bush that appeared to be burning but was not being consumed. As he approached the bush, God spoke to him. Moses was awe struck and frightened. He humbly asked God who it was that was speaking to him so he could pass that name on to others. God said, "I am who I am. This is what you are to say to the Israelites: I AM has sent me to you."[7] At first this appears to be a strange name for God, but in reflection it is perfect. The name provides a description that does not limit his nature, power or expanse. He simply "is." He is too big for any other name.

This God exists and is unlike any other being or thing. This God is outside of time and always in the present tense. God is self sufficient,[8] eternal,[9] spirit,[10] invisible,[11] alive,[12] omnipresent (present everywhere),[13] omniscient (all knowing),[14] and omnipotent (all powerful).[15]

False gods may be destroyed, lost or stolen. The true God of the Bible cannot.

---

[7] Ex.3:14.
[8] Eph.1:5,11.
[9] Ge.21:33; Ps.90:1-2; Rev.1:8, 21:6; 22:13.
[10] Jn.4:24; Lk.24:39.
[11] Jn.1:18; Col.1:15.
[12] Jos.3:10; Mt.16:15; 1Ti.3:15.
[13] Ps.139:7-10.
[14] Ps.139:1-10.
[15] Job.42:2; Mt.19:26; Jer.32:17.

God Defies Proof

It is impossible to conclusively or scientifically prove or disprove God. This is because God is a spiritual being living in a spiritual realm, invisible to our eyes and undetectable to our physical senses. You can't place God in a laboratory to run tests on him.

Additionally, God often defies predictability. The Bible describes numerous instances where God just doesn't act the way we think he should. In a culture that gave preeminence to the firstborn son, God often chose someone further down the line to lead the family of God.[16] At a time when many Jews thought God's precious temple would never be destroyed, God brought in a foreign army to destroy it, as if to say, your reliance on this physical building is out of line.[17] When Jesus' disciples expected him to rush to the side of his dying friend Lazarus, Jesus, as God in human form, purposefully remained away a few more days.[18] When some tried to trick Jesus into saying something that would offend either the Jews or the Romans by asking whether the people should pay taxes to Caesar or not, Jesus responded, "Give to Caesar what is Caesar's, and to God what is God's."[19] When some challenged Jesus by throwing a woman caught in adultery at the feet of Jesus he had an answer no one anticipated, "If any one of you is without sin, let him be the first to throw a stone at her."[20] Jesus frequently stopped people in their tracks because he said and did things that nobody expected. One can't try to prove or disprove God based on some expectation of how God will act, because God has a history of defying expectation.

---

[16] *The unexpected order.* God chose Jacob instead of Esau (Ge.27), Judah instead of Reuben (Ge.35-50), David instead of Eliab (1Sa.16-17), and Solomon instead of Amnon (1 Ch.3).

[17] *Unexpected destruction of temple.* Jeremiah warned against undue reliance on the temple (Jer.7:1-7). The temple was destroyed by the Babylonians in 586 BC (2Ki.25; 2Ch.36:15-21).

[18] Jn.11.

[19] Mt.22:21.

[20] Jn.8:7.

Yet, the evidence of God's design and existence is all around us. Paul told us the evidence for God is clearly seen.[21] The psalmist said the heavens declare God's glory.[22] All we have to do is look around at the complexity and beauty of this world and the life upon it to see evidence of God's masterful handiwork.

The human body is an amazing system of complex living parts. It can reproduce itself. It can even heal itself when attacked by minor injuries and illnesses. This body can adjust and adapt to differing conditions. The human mind has a capacity to learn and reason that is almost unbelievable. The systems and functions of the human body are themselves evidence of a great and powerful God who creates complex systems of order out of what would otherwise be chaos.

Even Albert Einstein, who was not a traditional believer, saw this amazing sense of design.

> Every one who is seriously involved in the pursuit of science becomes convinced that a spirit is manifest in the laws of the Universe – a spirit vastly superior to that of man, and one in the face of which we with our modest powers must feel humble. In this way the pursuit of science leads to a religious feeling of a special sort...[23]

The mathematical probability that all this could happen without God's design is so astoundingly low that it would take a tremendous speculative leap of faith to believe in such a theory.[24]

---

[21] Ro.1:20.

[22] Ps.19:1.

[23] *Einstein, His Life and Universe*, by Walter Isaacson, New York, NY: Simon & Schuster, 2007, p.388.

[24] Antony Flew's book, *There Is A God*, Harper One: New York, New York, 2007, pp.76-77, provides an example of the absurdity of the numbers one has to accept as the mathematical possibility that even very simple things could happen by chance. He references Schroeder's calculations on the mathematical chance that monkeys could put letters and words together

God in Three Forms – The Trinity

The Father, the Son and the Holy Spirit make up the God of the Bible. The "Father" is that being who lives in spiritual dimensions and whose dwelling place is heaven. The Son is Jesus, through whom the earth and all life was created, who emptied himself of divinity and walked on this earth in physical form for approximately 33 years, and then ascended to be with the Father in heaven. The Holy Spirit is the "breath" or "essence" of God[25] who is given to believers to equip them for ministry, work the miracles of God, and to transform people from the inside out. The Father, the Son,

---

in the correct order to create even one of Shakespeare's sonnets, with 488 letters, is 10 to the 690th. That is 1 with 690 zero's after it. ...He shows that even if all the universe were converted into computer chips and each chip was able to spin 488 trials at a million times a second producing random letters, "the letters you would get would be 10 to the 90th trials. It would be off again by a factor of 10 to the 600th. You will never get a sonnet by chance." Life is much more complex than a Shakespearian sonnet. Do you really want to put your *faith* in the chance that life happened by accident when the chances are so mathematically improbable as to be effectively non-existent? See also *The Case For A Creator*, by Lee Strobel, Zondervan: Grand Rapids, Michigan, 2004, pp.222-226.

[25] *Holy Spirit.* The term, "Spirit," comes from the Hebrew רוח (*ruach*) and the Greek πνευμα (*pneuma*). *The New Strong's Expanded Dictionary of Bible Words*, by James Strong, Nashville, TN: Thomas Nelson Publishers, 2001, p.808, §7307 רוח (*ruach*) & p.1321, §4151 πνευμα (*pneuma*). These terms refer to the "breath, wind, breeze, or spirit of some living being." They refer to the essence of that being. If the terms are being applied to the spirit of a human being, they are referring to the essence of that human being. When these terms are coupled with the term "Holy" and used without any further modification (ex. "Holy Spirit") they are automatically merged with God and refer to "the mind, energy and life of God." The Holy Spirit is the Spirit of God set apart for God's work, desires, and pleasure. This Spirit is the very essence of God and is personal in nature (Used with personal pronouns - Jn.14:26; 26:13-14 and exhibiting personal attributes.)

and the Spirit, are all personal in nature and are described with personal attributes[26]

Even though there are three personages of God - God is one.[27] The Father, Son and Holy Spirit work together as one. They are three persons and functions of the one whole. The Son and Holy Spirit carry out the work of the Father. The Holy Spirit is the replacement for the physical Jesus who only lived on this earth for one generation.[28] The Holy Spirit functions as the mind of Christ within for as long as we remain true to God.[29]

This three-in-one concept is often called "the Trinity." The term "trinity" is not found in the Bible. But the concept is clearly there as divine qualities are ascribed to each of the three and they all emanate one from another.[30] How this can be is a mystery, but then we are talking about a spiritual realm into which we are only given glimpses. Our physical laws do not govern the spiritual realm. The Bible speaks of three personages in one single God. Generally we think of the Father as the initiator, the Son as the visual representation of the invisible God, and the Holy Spirit as the power and force of God. All three are personages and not just forces.

Various people have provided analogies to help us conceptualize the trinity. Tradition holds that St. Patrick of Ireland suggested the "trinity" is like a three leaf shamrock. It has three separate leaves but all a part of the same shamrock. The trinity has been explained

---

[26] *The Holy Spirit's Personal attributes* - Lk.12:12, Jn.14:26; 15:26; Ro.8:16; 8:27; 1 Co.2:11-13; 12:11; 15:30, 1 Jn.2:27; Gal.4:6; 1 Jn.3:24; 1 Jn.4:13; 5:6, Jn.16:8-11, Jn.16:13, Jn.16:14, Ac.13:2, Acts 13:2; Rev.2:7, Ac.16:6f, Ro.8:26, 1 Co.2:10.

[27] Dt.4:35; 6:4; 32:39; 2Sa.7:22; 1 Ch.17:20; Ps.83:18; 86:10; Isa.43:10; 44:6; 45:18; Mk.12:29; 1 Co.8:4; Eph.4:6; 1Ti.2:5.

[28] Jn.16:7.

[29] Ro.8:9; 1 Co.2:16.

[30] "*Trinity*" Mt.28:19; God is one: Dt.6:4-9; 1 Co.8:4; Eph.4:6; Jas.2:19); God is three: Ge.1:26;11:7; Father as God (Jn.6:27; Ro.1:7; Gal.1:1); Jesus as God (Jn.1:1-2,14; 10:30; 14:9); Spirit as God (Heb.9:14; Ps.139:7-10; 1 Co.2:10-11), Lk.1:35) "Spirit"= "breath, life or essence of God."

as a flame in which there is a chemical reaction that initiates the flame (the Father), the orange visual flame (Jesus), and the energy or heat (the Holy Spirit). It's been described as an apple, with the core, the meat, and the skin – all three separate parts of the one single apple. It has been explained as the three roles of one person who can be son, husband, and father all at the same time. These illustrations may help, but none of them fully gets at the unique nature of the trinity of God.

God as Creator

God, as the creator of all good things, is also the one who sustains the universe and life itself. He is powerful enough to create a planet, a solar system, a galaxy, and a universe. He is also focused on the microscopic to the point of being able to create amoebas, atoms, quarks, leptons, and perhaps even smaller particles.[31] God is like an artist. Only instead of using paint, marble, or clay, he sculpts worlds and landscapes. As the master artist, he is able to create life in all forms, with people as his crowning achievement.[32] The complexity and beauty of the human body is absolutely amazing and can't help but bring a sense of awe to the observer. It is like marveling at a master artist's greatest work.

---

[31] *Genesis 1 theories.* There are a number of theories about how Genesis 1, describing creation, should be interpreted. (1) Some believe God created it all in six 24-hour periods of time. (2) Some believe the "day" image in Genesis 1 references eons or ages of time that might each be thousands or even millions of years in length. (3) Some believe there are gaps in Genesis 1 & 2 in which thousands or millions of years of events occurred. (4) Some believe Genesis 1 is simply a poem not written as a chronology of the creation process, but rather to communicate the fact that God is the creative author of all life with people as the pinnacle of that creation. Fact is, one could hold any of these views and still live a full abundant holy life in obedience to God.

[32] Eph.2:10.

God Does Not Change

We live in a constantly changing world, but there is one constant. God does not change.[33] God has periodically permitted or initiated changes in the forms of worship and service throughout time.[34] God doesn't always repeat the same actions over and over again.[35] But God's nature does not change. There is no change in his care for people, his aversion to sin, his desire to deal with sin, and his plan to give people eternal life with him in heaven. God is our anchor in a sea of change.

---

[33] Jas.1:17; Mal.3:6; Heb.6:17-19; Isa.40:8.

[34] *Change* in the form of worship and service to God has occurred throughout history. In Moses' day tabernacle worship and a formal priesthood was established for a nomadic people. In Solomon's day formal corporate worship revolved around a fixed location at the Temple. In 586 BC Jerusalem was destroyed by invading Babylonian armies who took most of the people back to Babylon as captives. The Temple was destroyed. Most scholars believe the synagogue form of worship began during this Babylonian captivity as an alternative to Temple worship. These were all *changes* in the form of worship in which the people engaged. We read about the beginnings of the church in Acts 2. At that point in time there were no appointed servants of the church. That *changed* in Acts 6 when we read about the appointment of the first church ministers or servants. Up through Acts 9, the church was Jewish in nature. We don't read about any Gentiles being baptized into Christ. That *changed* in Acts 10 with the conversion of Cornelius, a Roman centurion. Through the very early days of the church (through Acts 10), the followers of Christ were called by various names, but never by the name "Christian". That *changed* in Acts 11:26 at which time the followers were first called "Christians."

[35] *Unique actions.* God may never lead people by a pillar of cloud or a pillar of fire again (Ex.13:21). The parting of a sea (Ex.14) may not ever occur again. It may be that God will not raise someone again who was dead for four day (Jn.11), except in the final resurrection. I'm not aware of anyone turning water into wine (Jn.2) since the first part of the 1st century AD

God is Holy

God is holy, which literally means, that God is "set apart" from the general or common and dedicated to a particular purpose.[36] That which we see repeatedly in everyday life used for ordinary purposes is deemed part of the "common" or "general" world. A lamp that sits in my living room is deemed "common" because there are millions of lamps throughout the world that are either the same or similar. It is used for the general purpose of lighting whatever room it is in.

But there are some aspects of life that are anything but common. God is set apart from all others in a number of significant ways. He is completely unique. God is not part of the created world order, but rather the creator. God is different in that he is fully spirit and not physical. God always loves. God is completely and consistently true to his values. There is no other like God.[37] As such, God is considered "Holy."

A *person* is said to be holy when he or she is set apart from the world and committed to the Holy God of the Bible. The Greek term αγιος ("*hagios*") means the "set apart ones," but is often translated, "saints."[38] When used of people it refers to those who have committed to being God's servants to be used by God for his purposes.

---

[36] *Holy. The New Brown Driver Briggs Gesenius Hebrew and English Lexicon*, Christian Copyrights, Inc., 1983, §6944, p.871-872. "Be set apart, consecrated 1. Be set apart, consecrated, ...2. Be hallowed by contact with sacred things, and so tabooed from profane use, ...3. Set apart as sacred, consecrated, dedicate." *Ibid*, §6942, pp.872-873. *The New Strong's Expanded Dictionary of Bible Words*, by James Strong, Nashville, Thomas Nelson Publishers, 2001, §40 αγιος (*hagios*), p.909. "*Hagios* fundamentally signifies separated, and hence, in Scripture in its moral and spiritual significance, separated from sin and therefore consecrated to God, sacred."

[37] Ex.20:2-6; 1 Co.8:4.

[38] *The New Strong's Expanded Dictionary of Bible Words, Ibid,* §40 αγιος (*hagios*), p.909.

Even *things* and *animals* can be holy if they are set apart from the common and dedicated exclusively to God's purposes. The utensils made for the Jewish Temple were considered holy because they were made exclusively for God's purposes and not for common use.[39] Animals dedicated to the Lord were considered "holy."[40]

"Holiness" in people also implies a certain morality. God is holy in that he is light and there is no darkness in him.[41] He is sinless, meaning he does not fall short of his desire and design for himself. In fact, his nature defines what "sinless" means. It means *not* falling short of God's desire and expectation for one's life. As one might expect, this means that Jesus, the Son of God, part of the Godhead, is also sinless.[42]

God is Just

God is "just" in that he seeks what is right and fair.[43] He requires that someone who has done wrong or failed to be what he or she should be, must pay for that wrongdoing or negligence. It is like the sentence a court issues upon a finding that a defendant is guilty or liable. Sin brings consequences and sin must be addressed.

Justice is not the same as jealous revenge or vindictive retribution. Jealous revenge and vindictive retribution grow out of a selfish desire to hurt someone who has hurt you. The family struggles between the Hatfields and McCoys in the 1800's were the result of selfish retribution, not justice. One family member felt wronged and struck out in retribution against the other. The victim of that retribution struck back against the other. And so developed

---

[39] Ex.30:26-29; Ex.31:14; Nu.4:15.
[40] Lev.27:9.
[41] 1 Jn.1:5.
[42] Heb.4:15.
[43] Ps.103:6; Zep.3:5; Jn.5:30; Ro.2:2.

a spiral of selfish retribution that had nothing to do with justice or concern for the other family members.

Justice arises out of a concern for all humankind and the desire to help develop the right kind of heart in all people. Fairness and impartiality[44] are at the heart of this sense of justice. Those who do well are upheld and honored. Those who do wrong pay for their wrongdoing. This sense of justice is a part of the very nature of God. It's part of nature's balance. Wrongdoing hurts people and that hurts God. The consequences of wrongdoing, the sentence imposed on wrongdoers, is severe.[45]

God is Merciful

God is also "merciful."[46] Mercy means that God withholds punishment for our wrongdoing or negligence. God has compassion on those who stumble. He understands the struggle we face to remain true, good, and faithful. So God does not always dole out the punishment deserved.

At first glance this characteristic of mercy appears to be in conflict with the characteristic of being "just." Justice requires payment for a debt created by wrongdoing. Mercy is the forgiveness of that debt. But the story of Christianity is how these two characteristics blend together in Jesus Christ to make something entirely different from anything we see anywhere else.

God Permits Bad to Happen

Many have rejected the existence of God because they see bad things happening to innocent or relatively good people. "A good God

---

[44] Ja.2:3-4; 3:17; Col.4:1.
[45] Ro.6:23.
[46] Lam.3:22-23; Joel 2:13.

would not permit such a thing" is the reasoning. But this reasoning is contrary to the picture of God presented in the Bible.

The Bible teaches good and bad circumstances fall on good people and bad people alike.[47] There may be many different reasons why bad things happen to good people. Sometimes sinful people do bad things to others. Thus people, who are not led by God, hurt good people. Sometimes natural catastrophes or illness hit us with devastating force. But God is not necessarily the direct cause of these actions as if he were trying to arbitrarily punish people. One of the books of the Bible entitled "Job" is about a man by that name who is hit with a series of catastrophes. Job eventually learned that he was not to blame or accuse God, primarily because he couldn't see what was happening.[48] Job didn't know enough to understand the real cause of the catastrophes that came his way. Thus his blame of God flowed out of ignorance. James, the brother of Jesus, later warned we should not blame God for our temptations.[49] God is the source of good, not bad.[50]

Although God is generally not the direct source of our struggles, he does allow us to face tough situations. There is a reason for this allowance. James warned that rather than blaming God, we should understand that victoriously working our way through the challenges makes us stronger.[51] It is like an athlete who pushes his body through the rigors of training to become someone he could never become without the grueling experience of training.[52] It's

---

[47] Mt.5:45.

[48] *Bad on the good.* The Book of Job in the Bible begins with God granting permission to Satan to test Job, a good man, by bringing catastrophes upon him and his family. Job grows upset and accuses God of being unfair. Job wants his day in court against God so he can accuse God of wrongdoing. Eventually God responds to Job emphasizing how little Job understands about what is truly going on. Job repents and comes to understand it is not his place to question God.

[49] Ja.1:13-14.

[50] Ja.1:17.

[51] Ja.1.

[52] 1Ti.4:7-8.

like a Navy Seal who experiences the toughest training in life to shape him into a soldier who can accomplish almost superhuman feats.

It is also like someone who made it through some illness or hardship he or she did not choose who comes out the other end stronger and more courageous than before the hardship. It is these people who give hope to the rest of the world. It's a Helen Keller who can provide hope for others who cannot see or hear. It's a Corrie Ten Boom, who made it through the horrors of a German concentration camp in World War II, lost her father and sister at that camp, and was still able to inspire others to cling to God. It's a Lou Zamparini, who spent 47 days adrift in a raft after his plane went down in the Pacific in World War II followed by approximately two years in a series of brutal prison camps where he was severely beaten and starved. Years after his release, Lou forgave his cruel prison guard and searched for him to tell him so. It's a Nick Vujicic, a young man who was born without arms or legs, who inspires millions by helping them realize that if he can overcome his deficiencies, so can they. It's countless other people who's names are not found in books, movies, or newspapers, who make it through their own struggles and touch the lives of those around them. Seeing those who have had to struggle with unusually harsh challenges gives us courage to face our own challenges.

God uses the struggles in life to make us stronger. It is in the bad times that we realize we are not in control and draw closest to God. It is then that God can show us his love and strength better than at any other time in our lives.[53] It is at the roughest times that we tend to fully and honestly open up to God without any pretense or show. Here is where the relationship becomes real. It is in the tough times that we learn to trust God better than at any other time. It is the tough times that build faith in those who persevere with God.

---

[53] Ja.1:2-5.

Sensing God

During my early years as a Christian, while at college in Montana, our growing college church group would occasionally take weekend trips to a camp known as Bow and Arrow Ranch outside of Pray, Montana. You've probably never heard of "Pray, Montana," but it is about 22 miles southwest of Livingston and 30 miles from Yellowstone National Park. This tiny town is on the banks of the Yellowstone River at the Absaroka Mountains in Gallatin National Forest. The Camp was up in the surrounding Rocky Mountains at the mouth of the West Fork in Mill Creek Canyon.

At the time I started college there was a dirt road that led up to the camp. A small bridge crossed the river bordering the camp. Once on the campgrounds one immediately came to a main lodge and several primitive cabins, circling around an outside fire pit with benches for the evening campfires. Once I remember going up for a weekend and just living off of whatever fish we could catch. I have never been much of a fisherman, but I loved to eat what others could catch.

I used to wander off from the group, climb a long loggers road, and get to a point close to the top of the mountain. From that vantage point I could see not only down into general area of the camp, but also the tops of other mountains off into the distance. I was in awe sitting on top of the mountain. There were no distractions other than the overwhelming beauty and power of the creation I witnessed from that mountain point. It was just God and me. I would make up songs and sing them to God. Luckily there was nobody around with a recorder or the ability to put them on YouTube.

I realized this God I served was big enough to create all of the Rocky Mountains. He was artistic enough to shape them so that I, and others, could just sit for hours in amazement at their beauty. And yet, this God cared enough for each of those tiny people way down in the camp below, that they would never be left alone in this vast universe. God provided each of these people with the necessities of life and the ability to dream and hope. This unbelievably powerful creative God even cared about me.

I will always cherish those special times on top of that mountain where I could contemplate this God of the Bible. I could ask who he was, why he cared so much, and what he wanted of me. I could open up on top of that mountain and pour out my heart, my doubts, my love, and my praise for this wonderful God of life. God does permit bad things to happen to good people, but strength, courage, and maturity can grow out of persevering through the bad times.

Summary

A god is an object or being who is worshipped out of a belief that being or object has real power. The God of the Bible is unlike any other being. He is always present and all-powerful. God does not change. He is holy, or set apart from the common. God is both just and merciful, even though these two characteristics would appear at first to be in conflict.

Thought Questions

1. What characteristics stand out to you about the God of the Bible?

2. What most convinces you of the reality and existence of God?

3. Have you ever spent time contemplating God and his creation? What was that like?

4. What differences do you see between the God of the Bible and other gods?

5. What false gods are enticing to you? Why?

4

So Loved

For God so loved...

As an integral part of his very nature, God *loves*. He shows this love in his care for people.[1]

There were several Greek terms for "love" in the ancient world of Jesus. Most refer to the emotion and passion that can rise and fall depending on circumstances and moods. (1) Στοργη (*storge*) references family love.[2] This is the natural type of love one has for his or her own family members, especially one's parents or children. The Scottish Proverb, "Bood's thicker than water,"[3] grew out of the concept that there is a strong, almost magical, tie between family members. (2) Φιλος (*philos*) references brotherly or friendship love.[4] Friends are people, side by side, walking in the same direction, "absorbed in some common interest."[5] (3) Ερος

---

[1] Dt.7:8-9.

[2] C.S. Lewis wrote, "My Greek Lexicon defines *storge* as 'affection, especially of parents to offspring'; but also of offspring to parents." The *Four Loves*, by C.S. Lewis, Boston & New York: Mariner Books, 1960, Kindle Ed, Loc.371.

[3] *The Yale Book of Quotations*, ed by Fred R. Shapiro, New Haven & London: Yale University Press, 2006, p.609, Proverbs §31, from Allan Ramsay's *A Collection of Scots Proverbs (1750)*.

[4] *The New Strong's Expanded Dictionary of Bible Words*, by James Strong, Nashville, TN: Thomas Nelson Publishers, 2001, p.1439, §5384 Φιλος. "Friends"; *The Four Loves*, by C.S. Lewis, Kindle Ed., Loc.675.

[5] *The Four Loves*, Kindle Ed., Loc.722.

(*eros*) references the romantic sexual love.[6] This is love where two people are consumed with thinking about each other. Sexual desire is often, but not always, the result of this type of love. We might think of these three loves as "feeling loves" because they are feelings that naturally arise from relationships. But there is one more ancient term for love that is different from the other three.

(4) The term used here in John 3:16 for "love" is the verb αγαπαω (*agapao*).[7] The noun form is αγαπη (*agape*).[8] The term was infrequently used in the ancient world until the early Christians got hold of it and used it to describe God's love. This love is described by the Apostle Paul in 1 Corinthians 13:4-7.

> [4]Love is patient, love is kind. It does not envy, it does not boast, it is not proud. [5]It is not rude, it is not self-seeking, it is not easily angered, it keeps no record of wrongs. [6]Love does not delight in evil but rejoices with the truth. [7]It always protects, always trusts, always hopes, always perseveres.[9]

This kind of love is a *commitment* to *do what is best* for the other person. At any particular time the feeling loves may or may not be there. They rise and fall with circumstances and our own biological rythyms. The love of John 3:16 focuses on the *conduct* of serving the other person's best interest. It is action with the intent to help the

---

6   *Ibid*, Kindle Ed., Loc.1081-1112.
7   *The New Strong's Expanded Dictionary of Bible Words*, by James Strong, Nashville, TN: Thomas Nelson Publishers, 2001, p.907, §25 αγαπαω.
8   *Ibid*, p.907, §26 αγαπη. "It was an exercise of the divine will in deliberate choice, made without assignable cause save that which lies in the nature of God himself." ... "Christian love, whether exercised toward the brethren, or toward men generally, is not an impulse from the feelings, it does not always run with the natural inclinations, nor does it spend itself only upon those for whom some affinity is discovered. Love seeks the welfare of all, and works no ill to any."
9   1Co.13:4-7.

other person. It is *commitment* rather than passion. It's a decision, not an accident or coincidence.

Clint Black, a country music star, recorded a song that really catches the essence of this *agape* love.[10]

> It isn't something that we find ...
> Love isn't something that we have ...
> Love's not just something that we're in
> *It's something that we do ...*

Almost every commandment, encouragement, or reminder to love in the New Testament uses the same Greek term used in John 3:16 (*agape* as a noun and *agapao* as a verb).[11] This is a different love from all others, because it is not dependent on *feelings*. This makes sense because it is much easier to control conduct, than feelings. Feelings are not subject to command. God *can* command that we "commit" to someone a certain way.

> ²Live a life of love, just as Christ loved us and gave himself
> up for us as a fragrant offering and sacrifice to God.[12]

That is not to say that the other three loves (*eros, storge & philos*) should be avoided or have less value. They each have a purpose and a place. I am certain God has strong *feelings* for this world and its

---

[10] *Something that we Do*, by Clint Black, part of *Nothing But the Taillights* album by RCA 1997. Italics added for emphasis.

[11] *Love terms.* Most of the times one of the three feeling loves is used in the New Testament, it used as a description for the natural affection one feels for a friend, family member, or even the world. There are only a few times when some term other than *agape* is used in a command or encouragement to love. In those rare occasions, the term used always grows out of friendship love. Tit.2:4 = φιλοτεκνος (*philoteknos*) & φιλανδρος (*philandros*); 1Pe.3:8 = φιλαδελφος (*philadlephos*); Heb.13:1 = φιλαδελφια (*philadelphia*).

[12] Eph.5:2.

people. The words and conduct of God in the Bible evidence these strong feelings. Feeling loves are good and a natural part of life. *Agape* love is an important support for the feeling loves.

Agape love forms the foundation upon which all other types of feeling loves and virtues should be built.[13]

ερος *(eros)*   στοργη *(storge)*   φιλος *(philos)*
αγαπη *(agape)*

Agape love is what keeps the relationship going even when the other three loves wax and wane over time. *Agape* love also has a tendency to rekindle the other three loves when they lose steam. This is God's love – a selfless commitment to do what is best for the recipient of that love.

The Intensity of God's Love

The Greek phrasing makes it clear that John is emphasizing the intensity of God's love.[14] God's love is everlasting.[15] God's love never ends. Although God may be saddened, angered, or frustrated by our

---

[13] Col.3:14.

[14] "Theologians Gundry and Howell believe that the sense and syntax of the Greek terms Οὕτως…ὥστε make it likely that the author of the Gospel of John is emphasizing both (a) the *degree* to which God loved the world as well as (b) the *manner* in which God chose to express that love—by sending His only son. ….However, they add that the ὥστε clause that follows Οὕτως involves the indicative—meaning that it stresses an *actual* but usually unexpected result. They conclude that the sense and syntax of the Greek construction here focuses on the *nature* of God's love, addressing its mode, intensity, and extent. Accordingly, it emphasizes the *greatness of the gift God has given*." John 3:16, online at http://en.wikipedia.org/wiki/John_3:16.

[15] Jer.31:3.

rejection of him, our stumbling, our selfishness or our negligence, God continues to love us. He loves even when we continue to sin.[16]

God holds out hope for us and patiently longs for each of us to turn to him.[17] We get impatient with others, or even ourselves, when one fails over and over again. God's love means that he will patiently wait a lifetime to see us choose to become his.[18]

God adopts those of us who want to belong to him as his children because of his love for all people.[19] He actively *seeks* us out to adopt us as his children. He invites us to be part of his family. He tries to help us see the danger of not having a heavenly Father.[20] God brings those who choose him into his family with all the benefits and expectations that a parent would have of a child. He stays close by, sometimes standing just behind us when we don't really want him around, much as a parent would with an independent child who wants to do it himself or herself but is in danger of getting hurt. He carries us through when we don't have the strength to do it on our own.

However, God lets us go if we choose to walk a different path.[21] God can be very persistent in trying to convince someone to choose him. Jesus took Peter on a fishing trip he would never forget.[22] Jesus drew a Samaritan woman into a conversation that got her attention as no other would.[23] Paul's world was turned upside down by a vision of Jesus.[24] But regardless of the actions God undertakes to convince us to become part of his family and team, he does not *force*

---

[16] Ro.5:8.
[17] 2Pe.3:9.
[18] Mt.18:21-22.
[19] 1 Jn.3:1.
[20] Isa.1:5, 18.
[21] Ro.1:24-28.
[22] Lk.5:1-11.
[23] Jn.4:1-26.
[24] Ac.9.

anyone to commit to him. Rather, in great sadness, God let's the person who chooses not to walk with God, go his or her own way.[25]

God gave us life because of his love.[26] He infused his breath of life into humans to give us a spiritual nature[27] because of his love for us. He provides for us, comforts us and directs us because of his love for us. Our very existence is a testimony to God's love for us.

God has offered us forgiveness.[28] Regardless of how many times we stumble and fall, he offers forgiveness for all who choose to make him king and lord of their lives.[29] He offers forgiveness because he loves us. He doesn't want us to be estranged from him for some foolish decision on our part, or even a bunch of foolish decisions. He wants to help us grow into all that we can be. As such, he forgives and continues to work with all who commit to him, regardless of how many mistakes are made along the way.

Love comes from God.[30] We learn to love from God. The fact is, God is love.[31] Our very definition of "love" should first be defined by God's love for us.

God's Love for People

From the beginning God has demonstrated his love for people. The Bible tells the story of God creating a perfect home for Adam and Eve in the Garden of Eden. God provided for them and gave them all they needed, including purpose in life.[32] When they acted contrarily to God's instructions God remained with them. Adam and Eve had not discarded God. Rather they stumbled and fell for

---

25 Ro.1:24-28.
26 Eph.2:4-5.
27 Ge.2:7.
28 Ps.103:3; 130:4; Ac.5:31; 13:38; Eph.1:7; 1Jn.1:9.
29 Lk.17:4.
30 1 Jn.4:7.
31 1 Jn.4:16.
32 Ge.2.

a moment. They were cast out of the Garden as consequence of their sin, but God never left them. He knew they had not abandoned him.[33]

God revealed his plan for Abraham.[34] He was there with Abraham at every point of decision and challenge. He continued to work with Abraham even when Abraham lacked faith and told half-truths to save his own skin.[35] God knew Abraham was a man of faith who just got a little wobbly once in a while.

God worked with King David to shape the nation of Israel and led him step by step from the life of a shepherd, to being the greatest king of Israel's history. God refused to leave David even when David tried to conceal his adultery with Bathsheba.[36] He knew David was a man after his own heart who was briefly overtaken by his own selfish desires. David's words of repentance in Psalm 51 leave us a moving picture of the heart of this man of faith. God knew David's heart.

But it isn't just the faith *Hall of Famers* upon whom God pours out his love. God, the Father, has shown the depth of his love by sending his Son for *every* person on earth.[37] Jesus, as God incarnate, showed us the shape of God's love.[38] Jesus loved the important[39] and he loved the lowly.[40] He loved the sinful.[41] He showed the depth of his love by hanging on a cross so that each of us would have the opportunity to receive forgiveness.[42] It is interesting that another John 3:16, found in *1st* John 3:16, written by the same Apostle, also points us to the depth of Christ's love.

---

[33] Ge.3.
[34] Ge.12:1-3.
[35] Ge.12:10-20.
[36] 2.Sam.11.
[37] 1 Jn.4:10; Eph.5:2.
[38] Jn.15:9.
[39] The centurion in Mt.8:5-13.
[40] The beggar in Jn.9.
[41] Lk.5:8-10; 7:36-50.
[42] Jn.13:1; 15:13; Gal.2:20.

This is how we know what love is: Jesus Christ laid down his life for us. And we ought to lay down our lives for our brothers.[43]

God's love is so powerful that no external force can ever get between his love and us.[44] It is only when we give in to our *own* selfish desires, pleasures, or fears that we are separated from God. It is these actions that we choose for ourselves that get in the way of God's love and block our ability to see our loving heavenly Father. Evil and selfishness only have the power that we permit them to have in our lives.

The Apostle Paul says God's love compels us to respond.[45] To be compelled to respond, one needs to understand the nature and depth of God's love. This understanding usually comes from something more than just an academic reading of a description of God's love. It comes from experiencing his love first hand. Paul was in awe of how God loved him, called him and used him as an apostle in spite of the fact that Paul had initially rejected Jesus and severely persecuted Christians. Paul never forgot how God wouldn't give up on him. People like Paul are touched to the very center of their being in a way that compels them to move in gratitude, amazement, and wonder.

Love in Action

I have been the recipient of that amazing love of God. I met my first wife, Heather, while I was in college at Montana State University. We had both been very active in the Montana church. We married back East after I graduated and eventually moved to Lynchburg, Virginia where we rented a one-bedroom apartment and I worked

---

[43] 1Jn.3:16.
[44] Ro.8:35.
[45] 2 Co.5:14.

with a local TV station. We did some church hopping at first, but did *not* plug into any church. We never spent enough time with any church group to get to know them. Eventually we quit visiting the local churches and went - nowhere.

One night, a year and three months into our marriage, Heather slipped out of bed and headed to the bathroom. I was awakened by a crash down the hall. I sprang out of bed and looked out the bedroom door and saw Heather lying on the floor at the end of the hall just outside the bathroom. I rushed to her side as she lay unconscious. I could see she was struggling to breathe. I tried to force her breathing, but couldn't help. I called the operator. Soon the paramedics arrived. They ushered me to my apartment living room and went to work on her in the hallway. It wasn't long before one of the paramedics slowly walked out to me and asked if she had been sick. I asked, "Is she alright?" The paramedic sadly shook his head, "No."

The coroner came and our tiny apartment was filled with activity in the middle of the night as the paramedics and coroner did what they had to do. Then, after removing my wife's body from the apartment, they left. I was alone in the apartment in the middle of the night. I was really alone. I called my parents, who lived 180 miles away just outside of Washington, DC. Then I called Heather's parents who still lived in Montana. Finally I called the college minister who was at the Montana church my last couple years at Montana State University. This was a successor minister to the one who met me at the student center when I first became a Christian. We talked, prayed and cried on the phone. We hung up and again I was really alone. I couldn't sleep. I just sat there on my couch - all alone.

I think it was about 4 a.m. that I received a phone call. The man on the line identified himself as a minister of a church there in town. He explained that in the middle of the night my college minister in Montana had pulled out a church directory, looked up a church in the town in which I was then living, called the number in the directory and said, "We have a brother in need." The local minister didn't know my college minister or me. But he knew that I was hurting and he was going to reach out to me. He came over to my apartment and we talked, cried and prayed. Then he left – still before daylight.

About the time the sun was coming up I received another call. It was a woman from the same church of the minister who had just come over. She asked if she could bring breakfast. Then I received another call from someone else at that church. Then another. Then another. It seemed like the entire church had mobilized and was reaching out to me.

I was amazed. These people didn't know me. Yet, because of their commitment to God, by way of *agape* love, they reached out to me. It was all because a Minister in Montana called a Minister in Lynchburg and said, "We have a brother in need." This event helped me understand God's love in a new way. I have never been away from God or his church since.[46]

I know the church doesn't always work the way it should. Sometimes selfishness blocks God's love from motivating its members. But when the church works the way God created it to work, when God is allowed to lead, when *agape* love fills the hearts of its members, there is an amazing power in the lives of people.

---

[46] *Some may ask, "Why* would God allow my wife to die in the first place?" I can only speculate about possibilities: (1) We live in a fallen world filled with sin, disease, and catastrophes and God often lets events play out their natural course. (2) Perhaps God knew my wife was going to face a long painful demise and so he took her quickly. (3) Perhaps these factors, or others were working together. The point is, I don't know why God permitted my wife to die. I'm not going to blame God because of my own ignorance of the facts.

Summary

Selfless love is an integral part of the nature of God. God's love is never ending. Regardless of whether we are committed to him or not, God pursues us out of love. He will wait a lifetime for us to choose to be part of his family. God was even willing to allow his son, Jesus, to die on a cross, so that we might have real life, all because of love. God is love!

Thought Questions

1. Describe a situation in which you have been deeply touched by the love of one or more people, or by the love of God.

2. What do you know about God that leads you to believe he really loves you?

3. Why do you think God loves us so much?

4. Why do you think the members of a church would reach out to someone they didn't know?

5. What do you feel like when you are the recipient of someone's love?

5

The World

For God so loved the world...

God loves "the world." The Greek term κοσμος (*kosmos*) arises out of the concept of order or harmonious arrangement. It came to mean "the world" or "the universe."[1] It is the term used in the Bible to refer to the physical earth and all that is associated with it.[2]

The earth is a beautiful multi colored sphere that appears from a distance to change with each movement of the clouds. Blue predominates because of the amount of water covering the earth. The Apollo space missions of the 1960's gave us our first full view of the earth from outer space. It is the only known place of life encompassing nearly 9 million species.[3] The earth contains 57,510,000 square miles of land space and 139,440,000 square miles of water. You would have to travel 24,901 miles to travel around the earth at the equator. The volume of the earth is 260,000,000,000 cubic miles.[4] And yet, it is only a dot in the expanse of the universe.

---

[1] *The New Strong's Expanded Dictionary of Bible Words*, Nashville, NT: Thomas Nelson Publishers, 2001, κοσμος, §2889, p.1196.

[2] Mt.13:35; Jn.21:25; Ac.17:24; Ro.1:20.

[3] *Astronomy 101*, by Carolyn Collins Petersen, Avon, MA: Adams Media, 2013, p.42.

[4] *Earth Physical Characteristics Table*, online at http://en.wikipedia.org/wiki/Earth_physical_characteristics_tables.

All physical resources come from the world.[5] The very human bodies we live in are *of this world*.[6] They are composed of the physical elements of *this world*. Humanity does have a spiritual nature, but it is housed in a physical body. Thus the term "world" (κοσμος), at least in the John 3 context, includes the people who live on this world.[7]

God's World

God created the world. The opening verse of the Bible introduces God's message with,

> In the beginning God created the heavens and the earth.[8]

This creation includes not only the earth itself and what is on it, but also all that is within our solar system and universe.[9]

The creation is described in Genesis 1 is as if God was creating a series of great works of art. God figuratively stood back at the end of each stage, looked at his artistic creation and said to himself – "It is good." [10] The world's complexity, balance and striking beauty could only have come from the master artist himself. Man and woman are God's greatest artistic creations. They are the pinnacles of the creative process. Together they are God's masterpiece. [11]

---

[5]   Mt.16:26; 1 Co.7:31.
[6]   Ge.2:7.
[7]   Jn.7:7; 8:23; 14:30; 1 Co.2:12; Gal.4:3; 6:14; Col.2:8; Ja.1:27; 1 Jn.4:5.
[8]   Ge.1:1.
[9]   Ne.9:6; Job 26:7; Ps.102:25; Ac.14:15; Heb.11:3.
[10]   Ge.1:4, 10, 12, 18, 21, 25.
[11]   Eph.2:10.

People

Having grown up in the Washington, D.C. area, I used to love visiting the Smithsonian Institution National Museum of Natural History. You know – the one with the 8-ton, 14-foot-tall African elephant standing just inside the entrance. For many years there was a section in the museum that had a huge mural painted on one of its walls showing people of all different cultures with some of the dress and adorning customs of the people. It portrayed someone with tattoos, someone with rings around her neck to stretch her neck, someone with feet shrunken by wearing small shoes, someone with plates stuck in her lips to create a duck bill effect, someone with decorative items placed in the ear to stretch the earlobe, someone with big loops in the nose, someone who tried to mold her head into a certain shape, and many more customs. As I examined this mural it struck me just how different we are as a people across the world.

Seven years after the death of my first wife, I married Sharon, sent by God, whom I had met during Graduate school in Texas. A few years ago Sharon and I were riding the elevator up to the top of Coit Tower in San Francisco. This tower is on a hill that overlooks the city and the bay. As we were riding up the elevator, Sharon and I notice there were a number of other people speaking different languages. We counted and believe we heard seven different languages in that elevator. Again I was struck by how different we are as a people.

We humans come with variety. We live in more than 190 countries.[12] We create homes in five to thirteen different climate

---

[12] *Number of countries.* Figures range from 189 countries (*World Atlas* online at http://www.worldatlas.com/nations.htm), to 196 countries (*InfoPlease* online at http://www.infoplease.com/ipa/A0932875.html). In fact, the number changes frequently with shifts in the political landscape of the world.

zones.[13] There are about 6,500 languages in the world.[14] There are seven different types of governments under which we might live.[15] There are at least five different races of people.[16] Some people are heavily clothed, and some wear little or no clothing. There are 33 different human blood group systems running through our veins.[17] Some of us are tall and some are short. Some are thin and some are heavy. Some use every high tech gadget available as a part of normal life. Others lack high tech gadgetry altogether either due to unavailability or choice.

Yet, there are similarities that tie us together as one overall human race. God created each of us. We are all tied to this world while in our physical bodies. We all have to eat, sleep, and go to the bathroom. We all experience fear and we all need love. All human DNA is 99.9 percent identical.[18] We begin as babies, grow

---

[13] *Climate zones.* The amount of climate zones depends on the climate classification system that you use. There are several, but the most popular one in use is the Köppen climate classification scheme. It has five major climate zones that are divided in 13 sub-zones which themselves can again be split into finer groups. *Love Big Island Blog* online at http://www.lovebigisland.com/hawaii-blog/climate-zones-big-island/.

[14] *InfoPlease* online at http://www.infoplease.com/askeds/many-spoken-languages.html.

[15] Types: Democracy, Republic, Communism, Autocracy, Oligarchy, Theocracy, and Fascism. *Quizlet* online at http://quizlet.com/7037744/7-different-types-of-government-flash-cards/.

[16] *Races.* These are 1) Mongoloid (Asian and American Indian), 2) Caucasoid (European), 3) Australoid (Australian and oceanic), 4) Negroid (east African black), and 5) Capoid (south African black). *Yahoo Answers* online at https://answers.yahoo.com/question/index?qid=20061219212922AAx5JgV.

[17] There are four principal ABO types of blood: A, B, AB, and O. "A total of 33 human blood group systems are now recognized by the International Society of Blood Transfusion (ISBT). The two most important ones are ABO and the RhD antigen; they determine someone's blood type (A, B, AB and O, with + and – denoting RhD status)." *Blood Type* online at http://en.wikipedia.org/wiki/Blood_type

[18] *DNA.* "All humans are 99.9 per cent identical and, of that tiny 0.1 per cent difference, 94 per cent of the variation is among individuals from the same populations and only six per cent between individuals from

as children, and then move into adulthood (if we live long enough). As we move into old age our bodies slowly deteriorate. Eventually our physical bodies die. To be healthy we all need companionship, purpose and meaning in life. We all have the ability to become children of God.[19] God loves each of us more than we can possibly imagine. We are all "people!"

Managers of God's World

This world and all creation belong to God.[20] Everything *in* or *on* the world belongs to him.[21] *All* of it belongs to God.[22]

People are not owners, but rather managers of God's earth and its resources. Jesus tells a story of a man who was going on a journey and placed what he had in the hands of his servants.[23] They weren't simply to guard what they were given, but to use it for the owner's benefit.

Those who are given something in trust are required to be faithful to the owner.[24] In law they are called "fiduciaries." One who is appointed a fiduciary (trustee, conservator, etc.) has a legal duty to the one whom he or she serves. It is the highest legal duty in law. Using assets of the trust or estate of someone else for one's own personal desires brings serious consequences and severe penalties. The fiduciary has the legal obligation to administer the assets per the intent and instructions of the grantor (original owner). The fiduciary often takes a fee to enable him or her to live and pay the

---

different populations." *The Telegraph*, by Roger Highfield, Science Editor, online at http://www.telegraph.co.uk/news/worldnews/northamerica/usa/1416706/DNA-survey-finds-all-humans-are-99.9pc-the-same.html

[19] Jn.1:12.

[20] Ex.19:5; Lev.25:23.

[21] Ps.50:10; Hag.2:8.

[22] Ps.24:1.

[23] Mt.25:14-30.

[24] 1 Co.4:2.

bills of life. But he must not, for the sake of greed, take more than is reasonably required or authorized.

God's people have such a duty to the God of the universe to watch over the assets of the earth for God's purposes. We become God's fiduciaries. We use a portion of the assets under management to meet our needs of life. Some assets, like a house, may be used for multiple purposes including our own protection and safety, as a place to teach others about God, and as a place to provide shelter to others in need who lack housing. But we must never forget that our purpose, our task, is to manage God's earth and its assets for God's sake. Even our children belong to God as the master creator. We are briefly entrusted with their precious souls to raise them on behalf of their creator.

The End of the World

The Bible indicates that at some point in time, the world we know will end.[25]

> But the day of the Lord will come like a thief. The heavens will disappear with a roar; the elements will be destroyed by fire, and the earth and everything in it will be laid bare.[26]

All physical things associated with the world will end. The things we have stored up will cease to exist.[27] You may have seen the shows on TV in which a team helps someone struggling with clutter and hording clean out his or her garage, bedroom or home. What the team does at times seems severe. God's cleaning program is much more complete. The home I live in, the car I drive, the money I use to make purchases and pay bills, and the guitars that

---

[25] Mt.13:39; 28:20.

[26] 2Pe.3:10.

[27] Lk.12:19-20.

bring me so much pleasure will all either deteriorate with time or be destroyed by some cataclysmic event. Those things I would grab first if there were a fire in our house, like family photographs, will be gone. Even our present *physical* lives will end.[28] All physical things to which I have a tendency to cling will be gone.[29]

That ending of the physical life will signal the end of our chance to become a part of God's family. The choice for God must be made during one's physical life on earth. We each have one physical life to live and then comes judgment.[30] But not everything ends with physical death or at the end of our present world.

> [17]The world and its desires pass away, but the man who does the will of God lives forever.[31]

God's greatest creation – his masterpiece – humans - will continue on in a new form.

Summary

God loves the world and all that is in it as his own artistic creation. He was pleased to acknowledge that it was good. The creation of

---

[28] 1Pe.1:24.

[29] *End of the physical.* 2 Pet.3:10. Many believe that the physical world will be transformed, not destroyed. It will be renewed and God's original glory and purpose of creation begun at the Garden of Eden will be restored. This perspective comes largely from the Book of Revelation, which some take literally to refer to a physical kingdom established here on earth. *Rose Guide to End-Times Prophecy*, by Timothy Paul Jones, David Gundersen, & Benjamin Galan, Torrance, CA: Rose Publishing, Inc., 2011, p.74. I have taken the view that the Revelation passages of Chapters 21-22 are figurative pictures of heaven and not meant to be taken literally as the description of a physical city coming down from heaven to earth. One can live the full abundant life of God with either viewpoint.

[30] Heb.9:27; Lk.13:22-25.

[31] 1Jn.2:17.

people is God's masterpiece. They are priceless in value. God does all he can to care for and preserve his greatest creation so that people might spend eternity with him.

God loves his creation enough to undertake extraordinary action to save his greatest work. Just as a painter might run inside a burning building to save his greatest masterpiece from destruction, God acted dramatically, and at great cost, to save the people of this world from destruction.

This physical world is an amazing place and I love it. I marvel at God's masterful creation. Yet, I know it is the people who are God's master works of creation. It is people who are priceless in value. Our primary energy should be devoted to people, with the understanding that they are God's priceless works of creation. Any assistance we give to people is honor to God.

Thought Questions

1. What does "the world" mean to you?

2. In what ways does the earth and its people remind you of an artist's masterpiece?

3. Do you tend to focus more on the differences or the similarities among people? Why?

4. In what ways are people the managers, not owners, of this earth and all that is on it.

5. What danger exists in getting too attached to the world?

6. What do you view as temporary and what do you view as permanent?

6

That He Gave

For God so loved the world, that he gave ...

The phrase "that he gave" shows the result and consequence of God's love.[1] His giving is the result of his overwhelming love for all the people of the world – past, present and future.

God Gives

God is characterized by his giving. God *gave* the earth as a place to house people.[2] God shared his breath of life with humans to *give* them a part of his very own nature.[3] This gift provides us with the spiritual sense that allows us to understand, to some degree, spiritual matters.[4]

In addition to physical life, a home and a spiritual perspective, God further cares for us by *giving* his wisdom, knowledge and joy.[5] In fact, God gives wisdom generously to all who ask.[6] He encourages people to ask so that he can give whatever is needed.[7]

---

[1]   *A Grammatical Analysis of the Greek New Testament*, by Max Zerwick & Mary Grosvenor, Rome: Biblical Institute Press, 1974, p.292.

[2]   Ge.1-2.

[3]   Ge.2:7.

[4]   Ge.32:8.

[5]   Ecc.2:26.

[6]   Jas.1:5.

[7]   Lk.11:9.

God *gives* physical sustenance. He gives food,[8] sometimes to an individual and sometimes to large groups. He provides water[9] and rain.[10] He gives us the basic necessities of life for survival.[11] This is not to say that humans do not face shortages or famines from time to time. Rather it is to say that God is the ultimate source of what food, water and basic necessities we are given. Sometimes famines, floods, tornadoes, and deadly hail fall at God's command. Other times these events occur naturally as a consequence of the law of physics, the abuse of the environment by man or some other condition of the fallen state of life.

For some, God intervenes and heals diseases. The Bible describes people who are healed of leprosy, which in the ancient world was deadly, much like incurable cancer in today's world.[12] God has healed physical defects like withered or shriveled hands.[13] The blind have been given sight.[14] The lame have been given life in their legs.[15] Whereas some will always look for natural explanations for extraordinary events, God's people see his hand in these amazing tales of intervention.

We see examples in the Bible where God *gives* relief from demons that plague peoples' minds. Through Jesus, God drove out a demon that stopped a man from speaking.[16] He gave relief to a man who could not hear or speak because of the influence of a demon inside.[17] He healed a person who was so mentally disturbed that he would strip off his clothes and act like a wild man.[18]

---

8   Ex.16; 2 Ki.4:43; 2 Ki.17:14; Mt.14:15.
9   Ex.17:6; Nu.20:11; 2 Ki.3:16.
10   2Sa.12:18; 1 Ki.18:41.
11   2 Ki.4:5.
12   2 Ki.5:10; Mt.8:3.
13   1 Ki.13:4; Mt.12:10.
14   Mk.8:23; Jn.9:1.
15   Ac.14:10.
16   Lk.11:24; Mt.9:32.
17   Mk.7:33.
18   Lk.8:26-39.

God Does Not Rescue All from Struggles

God does not give healing for all of our infirmities or rescue us from all calamities. We can't really determine why God has granted some requests for healing and denied others. However, even denial of a request can show God's care, love, and graciousness. The great Apostle Paul was afflicted by some "thorn in my flesh,"[19] and was denied the healing for which he pled. Paul saw that denial as something good. God was protecting Paul's spiritual well being in denying the requested healing.

> [7]To keep me from becoming conceited because of these surpassingly great revelations, there was given me a thorn in my flesh, a messenger of Satan, to torment me. [8]Three times I pleaded with the Lord to take it away from me. [9]But he said to me, "My grace is sufficient for you, for my power is made perfect in weakness." Therefore I will boast all the more gladly about my weaknesses, so that Christ's power may rest on me. [10]That is why, for Christ's sake, I delight in weaknesses, in insults, in hardships, in persecutions, in difficulties. For when I am weak, then I am strong.[20]

Paul explains that, "suffering produces perseverance; perseverance, character; and character, hope."[21] Thus even God's refusal to remove the bad can be a gift of goodness.

---

[19] *Thorn in flesh.* It is uncertain what type of ailment Paul is referencing. There is great deal of speculation, but no certainty.

[20] 2Co.12:7-10.

[21] Ro.5:3-4.

God Gives Forgiveness & the Abundant Life

God gives forgiveness to all who trust in him.[22] This is one of God's greatest gifts in that it permits us to be reunited with God after our sin separates us from him. It is the gift that permits us to be adopted into God's family. It is the gift that gives us the hope of an eternal heavenly existence with God.

God gives us the *full abundant* life.[23] This is a life of love, joy, peace, patience, kindness, goodness, faithfulness, gentleness, self-control, compassion, and humility.[24] This is the result of permitting God to fill us with his Holy Spirit and lead us through life. It is not just a day-to-day physical existence. It is a life filled with purpose and power.

God's Gift of Help To Make It Through

God provides us with the strength to live his holy abundant life regardless of the circumstances in which we find ourselves. There are times when we are tempted by some person, situation, or stimuli which arouses our own desires to create a lust or greed that can be dangerous. But God provides help so that we can live his holy life in spite of the temptation. Paul encouraged us with these words,

> No temptation has seized you except what is common to man. And God is faithful; he will not let you be tempted beyond what you can bear. But when you are tempted, he will also provide a way out so that you can stand up under it.[25]

---

[22] Ps.Ps.84:11; 103:3; 130:4; Mt.6:14; Ac.5:31; 11:23; 13:38-43; Eph.1:7; 1Jn.1:9.

[23] Jn.10:10.

[24] Gal.5:22-23; Col.3:12-14.

[25] 1Co.10:13.

What we need to do is look for that way out.

There are times when we struggle to such a degree that we may think it is impossible to continue. God's call to a holy life just seems too hard. It is beyond human strength to remain true to God in these circumstances. I have often wondered how anyone could have survived the World War II German concentration camps like Auschwitz, Treblinka, Buchenwald or Dachau, or the Japanese prisoner of war camps like Ōfuna, Ōmori, and Naoetsu. These prisoners were deprived of virtually every physical thing they had. They lost family, dignity, and their health. Many lost their lives from cruel torture. It would be so easy to turn bitter and blame God. Yet some did remain true to God even in these harshest of circumstances. Acknowledging that we sometimes lack the strength to live the Holy Life of God in difficult circumstances, Jesus encouragingly said, "With man this is impossible, but with God all things are possible."[26] God provides us the means to tap into strength well beyond our own.

(1) *He has given us his Bible.* The Bible is a set of loving instructions on how to live the life to which God calls us, even when it is tough. It is filled with encouraging examples of those who walked with God. It is also a series of love letters that help us get to know God, the author. We should be reading his written word every day.[27] The Bible keeps us safe, steady, and solidly in line with God's desires for life. It also helps us maintain our focus on Christ as the center of life.

(2) *God has given us each other.* We call that team, the "church." The church is comprised of like people who are struggling with their own set of challenges. Although the challenges differ from person to person and in degrees, we all face life's challenges. As such, God calls us to encourage one another, so that each of us can make it through. "Let us not give up meeting together, as some

---

[26] Mt.19:26.

[27] Ps.1 & 2.

are in the habit of doing, but let us encourage one another."[28] Traditionally Christians have met on the first day of the week as a weekly celebration of Christ's rising from the grave.[29] Christians often meet together formally and informally at other times.[30] The difficulty of trying to live God's holy life is multiplied many times without the help of others. Meeting together with fellow Christians on a regular basis is an important part of obtaining that strength to make it through.

(3) *God gives prayer as a means to connect directly with him.* Prayer is open and honest talking with God. It can be done standing, sitting, lying prone on the ground, individually, in a group, spoken verbally, or shared silently. It can be done at particular times during the day or as small conversations with God throughout each day. We pray to ask for help or guidance and to give thanks and praise. We pray to build a relationship with God. We pray to ask God to show us how and where we can serve. We should be talking with God daily.[31]

(4) *He gives us his Spirit.* He provides us with his Spirit, a part of himself, who meshes with our own thinking to help us see life through God's eyes. God Spirit carries our prayers and heartfelt emotions to God even when we don't know how to pray.[32] With God's Spirit we actually have the very mind of Christ living within us.[33]

This is real power to help us deal with the difficult struggles we face. We can't necessarily change our circumstances, but we can live God's abundant holy life even in the harshest of circumstances with God's help and strength.

---

[28] Heb.10:25.

[29] Ac.20:7.

[30] Ac.2:46-47.

[31] Ps.55:17; 88:13; Mk.9:6-29; 1Th.5:17.

[32] 2Co.2:7-15; Ro.8.

[33] 1Co.2:16.

God Empowers Us for Ministry

God's Spirit does not simply indwell in our lives to provide strength and perspective in life. His Spirit is also *given* to empower us to carry out his mission and ministries here on earth.

> [7]Now to each one the manifestation of the Spirit is given for the common good. [8]To one there is given through the Spirit the message of wisdom, to another the message of knowledge by means of the same Spirit, [9]to another faith by the same Spirit, to another gifts of healing by that one Spirit, [10]to another miraculous powers, to another prophecy, to another distinguishing between spirits, to another speaking in different kinds of tongues, and to still another the interpretation of tongues. [11]All these are the work of one and the same Spirit, and he gives them to each one, just as he determines.[34]

God provides us with his Spirit to assist us in carrying out his work on earth. There is no finite ministry list into which we must fit. God's ministries and gifts are as varied as the people of all humanity. One's gift might be praying for the sick. It might be teaching God's word. It might be providing food and clothing to the homeless in the name of Jesus. It might be virtually anything that brings people closer to the God of the Bible. Most of us do not receive the power to undertake the miraculous (unless you consider any gift given by God a miracle), but we are all empowered to carry out whatever task God has given us.

God has a special place and ministry for each of us. Some of us are called to serve in multiple ministries. However, no one should harbor any expectation that he or she will receive any particular

---

[34] 1Co.12:7-11.

spiritual gift. It is *God* who determines how gifts will be dispersed depending on the ministry for which God calls his worker.

The Bible describes several basic principles of Spiritual Gifts. (1) They are given for the building up of the church.[35] (2) There are a wide variety of types of gifts,[36] (3) Each person is given one or more gifts.[37] (4) Gifts are given as God (not us) wills.[38] (5) We are to use our gifts for God's service.[39] Paul calls on us to eagerly desire the greater gifts,[40] which he describes as those that encourage other people.[41]

God Gave First

God *gave* before we did anything. He didn't wait until we demonstrated that we deserved to receive his gifts. God took the first step because that is the very nature of the one we call, "God."

God acted first to inspire us to also give. We know that if two people sit around waiting for each other to make a first move, that move may never be made. On the other hand, the giving of one person, motivated by love, will often inspire the recipient to reciprocate and give back to the initial giver, or even to pass the giving on to someone else. The phrase *"pay it forward,"* used as early as 1916, and later in a popular movie, refers to this concept that love shown to one person inspires the recipient to pass love on to others.[42] God knew about this principle long before the first human set foot on the earth.

---

[35] 1Co.12:7; 14:1-5, 12, 17, 26.
[36] Rom.12:6-8; 1 Cor.12:7-11; Eph.4:11-1.
[37] 1Co.12:7.
[38] 1Co.12:11.
[39] 1Pe.4:10.
[40] 1Co.12:31.
[41] 1Co.14:1-5.
[42] *"Pay it forward* is a term for describing the beneficiary of a good deed repaying it to others instead of to the original benefactor. The concept

We Give in Return

As a result of God's giving, we also *give* in like fashion. We are to give back to *God*.[43] There is no way we can ever repay God for what he has given to us. That is not the reason for our giving. Rather we give out of respect, love, gratitude and appreciation for God, and a desire to help in his work. It is the pure awe that we feel upon understanding the depth of God's love, as displayed in *his* giving, that compels *us* to give.

We honor God by giving *first* to him, before anything else. The Bible calls the gifts of this type, "firstfruits." We give a portion of our income to God first, before spending anything on ourselves.[44] We give in accordance with what we have been given.[45] We give without seeking self-recognition.[46] We are reminded that since we have freely received, we should freely give.[47] God encourages us to give from whatever we have.[48] Our time, our efforts, our money, and our focus should all be given first to God.

Our very lives should be shared with others.[49] In most cases we can't give what we have directly to God, who is not a physical being. Rather we give to other people in God's name, which is the equivalent of giving to God.[50] We are to look for and serve the needs of others. We give so that others may not be needy. We give to develop our own giving hearts. We give in ways that help others.

---

is old, but the phrase may have been coined by Lily Hardy Hammond in her 1916 book *In the Garden of Delight.*" *Pay it Forward,* online at http://en.wikipedia.org/wiki/Pay_it_forward. February 19, 2014. This concept is dramatized in the Warner film of 2000, "Pay it Forward" starring Kevin Spacey, Haley Joel Osmond, Helen Hunt and Jay Mohr.

[43] Ex.25:2; Nu.31:50; 2Sa.8:11.
[44] Pr.3:9.
[45] Dt.16:17.
[46] Mt.6:3.
[47] Mt.10:8.
[48] Ro.12:8.
[49] 1Th.2:8.
[50] Mt.25:40, 45.

Failure to serve the needs of others is evidence of a lack of love and a lack of generosity to God.

This is not to say that we *neglect* our families to give everything to the church entity or directly to others in need. Jesus warned against such an attitude.[51] Our families have needs too and they need our support. We are the primary ministers to our own families. Devotion and service to God should make us better at caring for our families. Giving in God's name includes caring for our own families.

Giving in Practice

I have been part of a number of giving teams. One stands out in regards to its impact on my family and myself. When our son was young, my wife, son, and I joined a team from our church that spent a week building a house for a poor family living in San Felipe, Mexico. I was told it would be very hot. I was told the people were very poor. I was told a great deal, but didn't really know what all this looked like until we got there. Each person from the team had to pay $80 for his or her own costs to make the trip possible (food, gas, etc). Remember this was decades ago when $80 meant more than it does today.

We headed down to Mexico from Campbell, California with many of the supplies we would need to build a house. We pulled into a local church in San Felipe, Mexico, where we had long helped support the minister, and set up camp. There was a large patio behind the church building that became our base. Adjacent to the open patio there was a partially covered outdoor kitchen and two small shower rooms without any man made light. There was just enough natural light to carry out the process of showering. Most of us slept at night on cots out on the patio under the open sky. The music from the cantina played into the morning hours, and then the

---

[51] Mt.15:3-7.

roosters started crowing long before daybreak. I thought they were supposed to start crowing when the sun came up! In the morning we would eat breakfast cooked on site, and then head out to work.

We each had assigned tasks. My wife was the group nurse and helped prepare meals in the kitchen. My young son was given a squirt bottle and his assignment was to keep us cool. I might be making bricks one day. The next day I might be working on the house itself. I'll never forget one day, while I was working on the roof, I looked around at the neighbors. They didn't have houses. They had lean-tos with sheets of metal, or plywood, or cardboard, or whatever they could find leaning up against some type of brace to form a very primitive house. Some would try to gather funds and build a house layer by layer. They might build one layer of cinderblocks and then run out of money. Thus most of the families that I could see did not have permanent structures for their homes. They didn't have electricity or running water. I had never seen poverty like this.

So we built a house. It was one open room just slightly larger than my living room. There was a door at each end and a window with glass on either side. The walls were the mud and cement bricks we made on site. It had no running water, electricity or gas feed. There was no heater inside. We dug a hole and put an outhouse on top of the hole out back. There was nothing fancy about it, but it was sturdy and watertight.

One of our men, Julius, who spoke fluent Spanish, was in town explaining that we Americans were there to build houses for some very poor people. One of the locals asked him, "How much does it cost to buy one of the houses you build?" Julius responded, "We don't charge for the house. In fact, we each have to pay $80 per person to come here to build the house." The locals were confused and astounded, "You mean you have to pay to build a house for someone else?" Julius nodded and explained that we were part of a church team and that each of us was dedicating a week to build a house for someone less fortunate than we were.

The last night we presented a local family with the keys to the house. This chosen family was called up to the front on that church patio as we all huddled close by. The keys were officially presented to the parents of this family. The parents were in tears. The mother gratefully said, "Now we have a house!" She was overcome by the wonderful gift we had given to her family. I was deeply moved to realize how much a simple little home like what we had built meant to this woman and her family. She finally had a house.

I have tried to be a giving person. We loan our personal property out to people who need it. We have loaned our van and SUV out over the years. We try to ensure that our house is frequently used for various activities designed to help others. I try to give of my time for projects designed to help other people. I give financially to church, charities and individual people. I want to be a giving person.

Unfortunately, I find a spirit of giving does not always guide me. Sometimes I am too attached to my own desires and things and too guarded of my own time. Sometimes I can be selfish. I wrestle with my tendency to spend money on my own desires without considering how God wants me to use what he has given to me. Sometimes circumstances beyond my control squeeze me financially making it difficult to give what I would like. Sometimes I unduly try to guard my time to the detriment of others.

I will never forget an incident that occurred years ago when I was working as a full time minister in Palo Alto, California. There was a young man with some mental deficiencies. He could function, but had trouble with social skills. He called me frequently to talk with me about his struggles. He needed help, but I grew annoyed with his calls. I finally said something that indicated he shouldn't keep calling me. He sadly asked, "If I can't call my minister, who can I call?" I realize one has to say "no" at times or be overwhelmed. Even Jesus went off from time to time to be alone.[52] But at that

---

[52] Mk.6:47; Jn.6:15.

moment, I had lost the sense of care and giving and had started looking at life through my own selfish eyes. Rather than seeing his needs, I saw the interruption. In fact, he was my work. I'm still a work in progress and I'm learning from God. I'm glad God doesn't simply see me as an interruption in his busy life.

Summary

Giving is a part of the very nature of God. It is not like God has to contemplate whether to give or not. He just does it.

Because of God's giving to us, we give to others. We give in response to the way God has given to us. It is not done to pay God back. It is done out of a sense of gratitude and wonder at how much God has given to us. We give out of genuine care for others.

Thought Questions

1. What physical blessings has God given to you?

2. What spiritual blessings has God given to you?

3. In what ways do God's gifts to you empower you to encourage or minister to others?

4. Describe a bad experience that turned into something good?

5. What touches you and reminds you that you should give more?

7

His One And Only Son

For God so loved the world, that he
gave his one and only Son...

A Parent's love

Because of God's love for the world, he gave "his one and only Son." Most parents instinctively know the deep love and affection that comes from having and raising a child. It is the cute little face, hands and feet that touch us with warmth that cannot be duplicated anywhere else. When they first say "da da" or "ma ma" our hearts jump. Hearing our children recite a first monologue, sing a first song on stage, or master the riding of a bike fills us with overwhelming pride. Even when they aren't all that we dream for them, they bring joy as we watch them mature. For most parents, they would willingly give of their lives, if need be, to protect their children.

Although we had taken a lot of pictures of our son, who was 11 years older than our daughter, it wasn't until our daughter was born that I purchased our first *video* camera. I have a degree in Film & Television Production so I was a natural to record virtually every historical moment of our family with one camera or another. The videos started with the birth of our daughter.

I remember how exciting it was to receive the news that after nearly nine months of pregnancy, our daughter was about to be born. I hurried to the hospital. Although I knew the way, in my rush I missed some turns. Upon arriving I quickly jumped in the first elevator door that opened and found myself in a service elevator that didn't go to the floor where my wife was waiting for me. I eventually found Sharon lying in a bed, hooked up to monitors, and waiting for the doctors to make their move. It was to be a "C" section because our baby daughter was transverse and could not be delivered naturally. They moved Sharon into the operating room and gave her a spinal block. She wanted to remain alert during the process so that I could be present in the delivery room.

So here is where it got cool. They brought me into the operating room and sat me down at Sharon's head - my videocam in hand. They started the operation and I couldn't really see much from where I sat because they had a sterile screen up between Sharon's head and where they were making the incisions to take the baby. Then the pediatrician who was present called to me, "Come over here so you can see." I got up to move to a position where I could see. Sharon expected to hear a crash as I fainted onto the floor. I did not faint. Instead I shot video and captured the birth. It was an amazing experience as our little daughter broke into the world to begin her life as our child.

Later in the evening I stood for a long time, with our son, and watched our little baby through the glass in the ICU Nursery. Each moment seemed so precious. The next day I was in the room with my wife and our son. I was able to hold our new baby girl. She was so small, so cute, and so amazing.

I shot a lot of video that first year. I wanted to catch each "first" on video. There was the first time she clutched my finger, her first smile, her first rolling over, her first "da da," her first sitting up, and her first steps. That first year video is still my daughter's favorite family video. As she grew I wanted to participate in each of her significant activities – her first song sung on stage, her plays, her soccer games, her birthdays, and her first experience on trips to see sights I had experienced years before.

I also shot video of our son on trips, at home, and anywhere else where there was action. I have video of his soccer games, his basketball games, his swim meets, and his water polo games. I can just hear him say, "On no, its dad with his camera again!"

A child is so precious to the person to whom that child belongs Whether born or adopted the child is loved as he or she becomes a real part of the family. One of the most powerful and protective relationships that exists is between a parent and child.

The most difficult thing for a parent to endure is the suffering or death of an innocent child. Parents don't expect to see their children die first. That's not the way it is supposed to work. So when a child, of any age, is struck with cancer, killed in a car accident, or murdered by the work of a heartless maniac, the parents suffer unbelievable heartache. It hurts so very much.

The hurt is magnified if the child who dies is an only child. There is no other child upon whom to pin a parents' hopes and dreams. There is no other child with whom to share that special parental pride and care. There is no other child upon whom parental nurturing and mentoring can be bestowed. There is no child to give back to the parents the love that only a child can give.[1]

Jesus is described as the "son of God." Jesus holds that special place of a son – an only son - in the heart of his heavenly Father.

Jesus, the Historical Person

In the flesh Jesus was a historical figure who lived from about 6-4 BC to about AD 29-30. He is evidenced by a host of ancient documents.[2]

---

[1]   This is not limited to just biological children. The death of a child acquired by adoption, foster care, or even a program like big brothers can be devastating.

[2]   *Biblical Archaeology Review*, by Lawrence Mykytiuk, Vol.41, No.1, Washington, DC: Biblical Archaeology Society, 2014, *Did Jesus Exist?*, pp.45-51.

The best known of these are the twenty-seven documents written between AD 48 and AD 95 collected together as our New Testament. We have a tendency to think of the New Testament as written by one author as if it was simply one book with many chapters. God is the underlying inspiration for the entire collection of documents.[3] But the New Testament (which focuses on Jesus) is also a collection of documents written by eight or nine different human authors, all of whom had belief and faith in this Jesus.

In addition to these twenty-seven documents of the New Testament, the Church Fathers wrote about Jesus. These are men who were additional leaders in the ancient Church. Clement, Bishop of Rome, wrote in the early AD 90's, about the same time the Apostle John was writing Revelation. Justin Martyr, Polycarp,[4] and a host of others followed Clement in writing about Jesus in the early days of the church.[5]

Ancient nonChristians also wrote about Jesus. Thallus, a pagan historian who wrote a history of the Eastern Mediterranean, mentions there was darkness the day Christ died (AD 50).[6] Mara Bar-Serapion, "an Assyrian Stoic philosopher in the Roman province of Syria," compared Jesus to Socrates (AD 70).[7] Flavius

---

[3] 2Ti.3:16; 2Pe.1:21.

[4] A young Irenaeus heard Polycarp describing his conversation with John. *Dictionary of the Christian Church*, ed. By J.D. Douglas, Grand Rapids, Michigan: Zondervan Publishing House, 1978, p.791.

[5] The early Christian leaders who came after the Apostles are known as "The Church Fathers." There are a number of books and collections that contain their writings. There are single volume summaries of the writings of the Church Fathers like *The Fathers of the Church* by Mike Aquilina, and there are the 38 volume sets like *The Early Church Fathers* edited by Alexander Roberts, James Donaldson, and Henry Wace which include the full texts of the Church Fathers.

[6] *Thallus,* http://en.wikipedia.org/wiki/Thallus_(historian) - Thallus was a historian who wrote in Koine Greek about 20 years after the crucifixion of Jesus.

[7] *Syriac MS in British Museum. Additional 14.658,* quoted in *Chronological and Background Charts of the New Testament*, Grand Rapids: Zondervan

Josephus, who was a Jew and the official Roman historian, wrote about Jesus with deep respect (AD 93).[8] Rabbis made reference to him. The Babylonian Talmud, a central writing of rabbinical Judaism, included several references to Jesus and Christianity (AD 70-200) [9] Pliny the Younger, "a lawyer, author, and magistrate of Ancient Rome," wrote to the Emperor Trajan and described the Christians and Christ (AD 110).[10] Tacitus, "a senator and a historian of the Roman Empire," wrote about Jesus (AD 115-117).[11] Suetonius, "a Roman historian belonging to the equestrian order who wrote during the early Imperial era of the Roman Empire," identified Jesus as the cause of problems with the rule of his followers (AD 120).[12] All of this ancient attention is absolutely amazing when one considers that Jesus had no political power, no military might, no monetary wealth, no Roman royal blood, and nothing that would ordinarily inspire so many writings.

There is actually more and better early evidence for the existence of Jesus than there is for Plato, Socrates and Aristotle all three put together. It is not the historian who doubts the existence of Jesus.

Publishing House, 1981 p.78. M*ara bar Serapion,* online at http://en.wikipedia.org/wiki/Mara_bar_Serapion.

[8] Jewish Antiquities 18.63-64, quoted in *Chronological and Background Charts of the New Testament*, Grand Rapids: Zondervan Publishing House, 1981 p.76

[9] *Sanhedrin 43a*, quoted in *Chronological and Background Charts of the New Testament*, Grand Rapids: Zondervan Publishing House, 1981 p.77. *Talmud,* online at http://en.wikipedia.org/wiki/Talmud.

[10] *Epistles 10. 96 "Letter to Trajan,"* quoted in *Chronological and Background Charts of the New Testament*, Grand Rapids: Zondervan Publishing House, 1981 p.77. *Pliny the Younger,* online at http://en.wikipedia.org/wiki/Pliny_the_Younger.

[11] *Annals 15.44*, quoted in *Chronological and Background Charts of the New Testament*, Grand Rapids: Zondervan Publishing House, 1981 p.78. *Tacitus,* online at http://en.wikipedia.org/wiki/Tacitus.

[12] *Life of Claudius 16.2 & 25.4,* quoted in *Chronological and Background Charts of the New Testament*, Grand Rapids: Zondervan Publishing House, 1981 p.78. *Suetonius,* online at http://en.wikipedia.org/wiki/Suetonius.

Jesus, the Son of God

Spiritually, however, Jesus was much more than a historical figure. He was the "Word, " the "Lamb," and the "Son" of God. The Gospel of John begins by describing the "Word of God."[13] The Word of God is the means by which God makes things happen. God's Word created the world and all its parts.[14] God provides direction for his followers by means of his Word.[15] God's Word has power to change things.[16]

John then clearly identifies this "Word" with the person of Jesus.

> [14]The Word became flesh and made his dwelling among us. We have seen his glory, the glory of the One and Only, who came from the Father, full of grace and truth. [15]John testifies concerning him. he cries out, saying, "This was he of whom I said, 'He who comes after me has surpassed me because he was before me.'" [16]From the fullness of his grace we have all received one blessing after another. [17]For the law was given through Moses; grace and truth came through Jesus Christ. [18]No one has ever seen God, but God the One and Only, who is at the Father's side, has made him known.[17]

Jesus frequently identified God as his Father.[18]

---

[13] Jn.1:1-5.

[14] Ge.1:3, 6, 9, 14, 20 & 24.

[15] 1Ti.3:16.

[16] Isa.55:11.

[17] Jn.1:14-18.

[18] *Father.* Mt.7:21; 10:32-33; 11:25-26; 12:50; 15:13; 16:17; 18:10; 18:19; 18:35; 20:23; 25:34; 26:39-42; Lk.22:29; 22:42; 23:34; 23:46; 24:49; Jn.1:20-23; 5:17; 6:32; 6:37; Jn.8:19; 8:54; 10:17-18; 10:29; 10:37; 12:26; 14:7; 1:20-23; 15:23-24; 16:23-25; 16:32; 17:1; Rev.2:27; 3:5; 3:21.

³⁶Why then do you accuse me of blasphemy because I said, 'I am God's Son'? ³⁷Do not believe me unless I do what my Father does. ³⁸But if I do it, even though you do not believe me, believe the miracles, that you may know and understand that the Father is in me, and I in the Father."[19]

In fact, the Father, the Son, and the Holy Spirit are all different personages of the same Godhead. As discussed earlier, this *three in one* is called the "Trinity." The three are repeatedly grouped together and interchanged. The Father is God.[20] Jesus is God.[21] The Spirit is God.[22] Jesus himself spoke of being one with the Father.[23]

And yet, they are distinct. The Father sends the son.[24] The Son speaks for the Father.[25] The Father loves the Son and the Son loves the Father.[26] The Father and the Son count as two witnesses.[27] The Father and Son glorify each other.[28] The Son is our advocate before the Father.[29] Jesus is the son of the Father.[30] Jesus prayed to the Father.[31] He listened to the Father for guidance and direction.[32] Over and over again, Jesus called God his Father.

---

[19] Jn.10:36-38.

[20] Jn.6:27; Ro.1:7; Gal.1:1.

[21] Jn.1:1-2,14; 10:30; 14:9.

[22] *Spirit as God.* Everlasting Heb.9:14; omnipresence P.139:7-10; omniscience 1 Co.2:10-11, omnipotence Lk.1:35.

[23] Jn.17:20-21.

[24] Gal.4:4; 1Jn.4:14.

[25] Jn.8:28; 12:49.

[26] Jn.3:35; 5:20; 14:31.

[27] Jn.5:31-37; 8:16-18.

[28] Jn.17:1, 4, 5.

[29] 1Jn.2:1.

[30] 2Jn.3.

[31] Jn.11:41-42.

[32] Mt.26:39.

Jesus, as part of the Godhead and the image of God,[33] emptied himself of divinity to become a human being.[34] The divine was given birth as a human with all the physical frailties that come from being human. Although retaining, at least in some form, the mind and attitude of God, he gave up his purely spiritual nature to live in this physical world. Jesus is called the "Son of God." The heavenly Father himself called Jesus his son.[35] Likewise Satan called him the "son of God."[36]

God the father had the same types of feelings and love at the physical birth of his son and throughout Jesus' earthly life as we do for our children. God sent out notice of the amazing birth of his son with great excitement to shepherds,[37] to wise men from the East,[38] to a faithful old man of God,[39] and to a prophetess.[40] Upon Jesus' graduation from life training as a Jew and carpenter, and entry into his full time work of preaching and teaching, God announced again how proud he was of his son.[41] As Jesus performed his ministry with determination and sacrificial giving, the Father again expressed how proud he was of his son at the transfiguration.[42] These were the expressions of a proud loving Father.

God Gave His Son

Yet as deeply as God cared for his only son, he gave his son to the people of earth. First, he sent his son to be born of a woman and to

---

[33] Col.1:15.
[34] Phil.2:6-11, 2 Co.8:9.
[35] Mt.3:17.
[36] Mt.4:3-6.
[37] Lk.2:8-15.
[38] Mt.2:1-2.
[39] Lk.2:25-26.
[40] Lk.2:36-38.
[41] Lk.3:21-22.
[42] Lk.9:28-35.

break into this world as a human being. In the familiar Christmas story, the angel, Gabriel, came to Mary and explained she was to become pregnant by the Holy Spirit. Joseph took Mary to be his wife and the two of them were required to travel to Bethlehem to register for a census. The baby Jesus was born and placed in a manger, a feeding trough for animals. Joseph, Mary and baby Jesus were then visited by shepherds and eventually some magi, or wise men.[43]

Second, God gave his son to *serve* the world. At around age 30, Jesus turned to full time preaching and teaching about the Kingdom of God.[44] For approximately 3½ years, Jesus wandered throughout Israel teaching people about the character and love of God and the nature of God's kingdom.[45]

Third, God gave his son to suffer and die on a cross to save our souls. At approximately 33 years of age, Jesus was arrested, tried before a mockery of a court, whipped, crucified,[46] and killed. God knew Jesus had to suffer to accomplish the important work of the redemption of people, but that knowledge could not possibly have eliminated God's pain of watching the suffering of his only Son. Can you imagine the sadness in God's heart at that dark moment? Can you imagine the depth of the love God has for us, that he permitted

---

[43] Lk.1; Mt.2.

[44] Lk.3:23.

[45] *Length of Jesus' ministry.* Most think Jesus' public ministry took about 3½ years. John the Baptist began his preaching in AD 26 in the 15th year of Tiberius Caesar's rule (Lk.3:1). Jesus probably began his ministry shortly thereafter at age 30 (Lk.3:23). Jesus attended three or four annual Passover celebrations (Jn.2:13; 6:4; 11:55-57 with one more possible between chapters 2 and 6). Considering the events described before, around and after those Passovers, most conclude the public ministry of Jesus lasted about 3½ years.

[46] *The cross.* Nailed or tied to a wooden pole with a cross bar. This was a common form of execution for those convicted of serious crimes. Roman citizens could not be crucified.

the activities of that cruel night and morning?[47] As horrible as these events were, they are crucial to the nature of the Good News of Jesus Christ.[48]

Why Did he Have to Suffer and Die?

Jesus was the only one who could ever have served as humanity's savior and he could only do that by giving his life as a ransom for us.[49] There is no other being who could fulfill our need for inspiration, guidance, perfection, justice, and atonement. Jesus is the only one who can fulfill all these needs in one person.

(1) Jesus serves as our inspiration. He is one who has been there before. He inspires us to live Godly lives because he made it through. Jesus walked the human life, encountered temptation, and wrestled with the struggles of life. Yet after facing the full force of temptation, including the cruelty at his trial and death, he remained sinless.[50] The words of one who has been through trials have much more credibility and power than the words of one who hasn't.

In 1968 Martin Luther King Jr. was assassinated in Memphis, Tennessee. Riots broke out in several places in which large populations of African Americans lived. Their greatest advocate had been assassinated. Robert Kennedy was campaigning for president in Indianapolis, Indiana and was to meet a large group of mostly African Americans as part of his campaigning. Against the advice of his advisors, who thought the situation dangerous for a white man, Robert Kennedy chose to meet with this group and

---

[47] *Bad things.* People are not the only ones who suffer the consequences and pain of bad things happening to good people. God was himself the recipient of the harsh cruelty that was poured out on his Son. Jesus was tortured for trying to help people. God knows what it feels like to hurt at the hands of cruel people.

[48] 1 Co.15:3.

[49] Heb.2:14-18; Ac.4:12; Jn.14:6.

[50] Isa.53:11; 2 Co.5:21; Heb.4:15; 1Pe.2:22; 1 Jn.3:5.

talk with them about Martin Luther King's shooting. A podium and public address system were set up so that Kennedy could address the crowd. When he stepped up to the podium Kennedy talked with them about King's death. He then said,

> For those of you who are black and are tempted to be filled with hatred and mistrust of the injustice of such an act, against all white people, I would only say that I can also feel in my own heart the same kind of feeling. I had a member of my family killed, but he was killed by a white man.[51]

The crowd relaxed. They knew Robert Kennedy had worked exhaustively for civil rights. They also knew that he had felt the loss caused by political assassination – the assassination of his brother, John F. Kennedy. Whereas others would not have been able to calm the anger of the group, Robert Kennedy could. Kennedy had been there, knew what they experienced, and could lead them through. Likewise, Jesus' words have credibility because he faced the struggles and hardships of life and made it through. It is this fact that inspires us to do the same.

(2) Jesus serves as our guide. He is like a pioneer who found a way through the challenging terrain and came back to lead others through. His earthly life showed us what obedience looks like even when obedience runs contrary to our own desires.[52] While most of us can resist temptation at times, not one of us can say we have lived in complete obedience to God at every turn of life. Jesus can.

Whereas Jesus appears to have been naturally aligned with the Father's will and desires throughout his earthly life, there is one exception. In the Garden of Gethsemane, just hours before his death, Jesus prayed that he would not be subjected to the terrible torture,

---

[51] *American Rhetoric*, online at http://www.americanrhetoric.com/speeches/rfkonmlkdeath.html.

[52] Heb.5:8-10.

loneliness and horror that awaited him that night. He anguished over this in prayer. However, he also committed himself to the Father's will and finished his prayer with, "not my will, but yours be done."[53] Jesus bent his will to that of the Father. As a result of Jesus' commitment to do God's Will, Jesus faced horrific suffering, the likes of which most of us will never know. Yet he remained sinless – and even forgave those who were so cruel to him while he was hanging on a cross and dying.[54] Jesus found a way through the challenges of life by being obedient to his Father at every possible turn. He was able to bend his will to the Father's. We can follow in Jesus' steps and make it through.

(3) He destroyed death's hold on those who follow him. Death is pictured in the Bible as a type of subterranean prison. His resurrection broke the spiritual bars that held him prisoner in death.[55] He didn't just escape. He destroyed the bars of one of the gates to this spiritual prison. Jesus knows the way out. He made it out. All we have to do, is trust and follow him to escape the clutches of death.

(4) Jesus resolved the problem caused by sin. Because of his sinless nature,[56] Jesus was able to offer his life in place of ours as a ransom for our sin. He could give his life for us because he did not need to offer his own life for his own sins.[57] Thus he used his life as a sacrifice for us to pay the sentence imposed on us for our own sins. Now our task is to unite with Christ and accept his sacrificial offering made on our behalf.[58]

---

[53] Lk.22:39-44.

[54] Lk.22:34.

[55] 1 Pet.3:19-22; Rev.1:18.

[56] Isa.53:11; 2 Co.5:21; Heb.4:15; 1Pe.2:22; 1 Jn.3:5.

[57] Heb.7:27.

[58] Ac.2:38; Ro.6:1-5; 10:12-13.

Substitutionary Sacrifice

To fully understand why Jesus had to shed blood and give up his life for us, one needs to understand something of the nature of sin and its consequences. In today's world there are many who believe there is no such thing as "sin." But "sin" is a central theme in both the Old Testament and New Testament. It creates havoc and disaster in the lives of people and it is the primary reason why everyone on earth needs Jesus.

"Sin" is "missing the mark" and "falling short" of what God wants in our lives.[59] It is making wrong choices. It is wrongdoing. It is failing to let God lead. The natural spiritual consequence of sin – is death.[60]

The Bible pictures life as being in the blood of a creature.[61] Even today we understand that excessive blood loss will sap the life from the human body. Blood drives are a familiar sight to ensure that hospitals have all different types of blood available when needed. We stock pile blood because it is so necessary to life. In the ancient world, blood was the symbol of life itself.

When someone was executed for a crime, the death sentence most commonly involved the shedding of blood. In our softer modern world, the death sentence is only imposed on the most brutal or heinous of the criminal population. Some believe the death sentence should never be imposed. But in the ancient world, the death sentence was a natural part of the legal system and was imposed for a vast array of crimes. Additionally God, who knows the destructive nature of sin, has an intense aversion to sin. Therefore it was natural for God to use the death analogy to help us understand that sin results in spiritual death and a separation from

---

[59] *"Sin"* = The Greek term means, "missing the mark." The Bible describes it as "falling short" of God's call to perfection – Mt.5:48; Ro.3:23)

[60] Ro.6:23.

[61] Lev.17:11 & 17:14.

God and his life. The consequence of, or sentence for, sin is death[62] and eternal separation from God.

"Atonement" is making amends for sin. One makes amends or achieves atonement for sin by the paying off the debt or fulfilling the sentence. The sentence must be carried out. Thus since death is the sentence for sin, only a death can fulfill the sentence and atone for the sin. The sentence must be paid.

In the Old Testament, to teach people about the nature of sin and salvation, God gave the Israelites a way to achieve atonement for certain wrongs without taking the life of the actual wrongdoer. The wrongdoer could sacrifice the life of an *unblemished animal* in place of sacrificing his own life.[63] With the debt paid by another, the sins of the actual sinner were deemed forgiven.[64]

The sacrificial animal was to be *without defect.*[65] It was to be *perfect.* God calls *us* to perfection as the standard for salvation.[66] Only one who does *not* fall short of God's glorious ideal can serve as a substitutionary sacrifice for the wrongdoer who does fall short. A flawed person could not sacrifice for others, because he would first have to give his own life for his own sin.

In reality, the Old Testament model of shedding the blood of an *animal* for atonement of the wrongdoer's sin was *not* to achieve actual forgiveness, but rather to demonstrate the need for an unblemished creature's blood to achieve atonement.[67] No *animal* can fulfill the sentence imposed on a hu*man being.* Only a spiritually unblemished, perfect, *human being* can fulfill the sentence of another *human being.* The Bible makes it clear that there is only one human being who is unblemished (sinless). That is Jesus Christ.[68]

---

[62] Ro.6:23.

[63] Lev.17:11; Heb.9:22.

[64] Lev.4-6; 16.

[65] Ex.12:5; Lev.1:3; 1:10; 22:21.

[66] Mt.5:48.

[67] Gal.3:19-22; 1Pe.1:10-12; Heb.10:1-4.

[68] Isa.53:11; 2 Co.5:21; Heb.4:15; 1Pe.2:22; 1 Jn.3:5.

Jesus served as the only truly effective substitutionary sacrifice for *people*.[69] The sin of the world was placed on Jesus' shoulders as he took on our spiritual debt.[70] Jesus became the debtor in our place. When he took on our sins, God, the Father, saw Jesus as the sinner instead of us. As such when Jesus was dying on the cross, bearing the sins of the world, he was in great anguish over his resulting separation from God, the Father. Jesus cried out from the cross in a loud voice, "My God, my God, why have you forsaken me?"[71]

In contrast, when God now looks at the sinner who has accepted Christ's sacrifice, God sees no sin. All of the sin has been transferred to Jesus. Jesus gave his life in payment of the debt or the sentence owed by you and me. Just before he died, Jesus said, "It is finished."[72] The sentence was fulfilled. The debt was paid. Atonement had been made – all by the blood of Jesus. The actual wrongdoer is completely forgiven. This is what makes the restored relationship between humans and God possible. The blood of Jesus even covers those who had relied on animal sacrifices, which served as a type of placeholder for the real sacrifice of Jesus. Here is where reconciliation occurs.[73]

The Loss of a Child

I have never personally experienced the loss of child to tragic death, but others have. On October 1, 1993 twelve-year-old Polly Klaas was kidnapped during a slumber party at her home in Petaluma, California. She was abused and then strangled. Richard Allen Davis

---

[69] Heb.10:1-6.

[70] Gal.1:4; Eph.5:2; Tit.2:14; 1 Jn.3:16; Rev.1:5; Jn.10:11; Ro.5:6; 1 Co.15:3; 2 Co.5:15; Rev.5:9.

[71] Mt.27:46.

[72] Jn.19:30.

[73] 1Pe.3:18.

was convicted of her murder in 1996. At the end of the trial he mocked the court and made snide comments about sexually abusing Polly. Can you imagine how Polly's father felt sitting in court, watching the antics of this man consumed with evil, and listening to those cruel confessional statements of abuse perpetrated on his innocent daughter? Perhaps this gives us some sense of the emotional impact God felt at the cruel unjustified death of his son and the mocking insults made by some as Jesus hung on the cross struggling for breath.

Why would God permit his son to empty himself of divinity, live the harsh life of a physical human, be arrested, tortured, mocked and executed on a cross? The Bible explains God gave his son to us because of his "love" for us. What a tremendous gift arising from an extraordinary love for you and me. When I think about it, I am completely awed.

Summary

Jesus is the only one who can give his life as ransom for us, because he is the *only* human (1) who has experienced the temptations of life without falling to his own selfish desires, (2) who has successfully navigated a path through life without falling short and can therefore guide us through, (3) who overcame the clutches of death, and (4) who does not need to pay the price for his own sin with his own life. He is, in the words of the Old Testament requirements for sacrifice, "unblemished." Thus he has no obligation to pay any debt or any sentence to God for his own sins. He can instead give his life as a ransom for us.

It is for these reasons, and probably many more, that God gave Jesus to be born of a woman, to undertake his preaching ministry, and to suffer and die on a cross. This made it possible for you and me to put our trust in what God has done for us to overcome sin, death, and despair. God's gift of his son made salvation for humankind possible.

Thought Questions

1. What makes a parent's love so strong?

2. Some of the stories about Jesus are pretty amazing. What reasons do you have to believe the credibility of these stories?

3. What did Jesus go through that helps you believe that Jesus has been through the type of struggles you have faced?

4. How do you think God felt during the trial and crucifixion of Jesus?

5. In what ways is Jesus the perfect savior for you?

8

That Whoever

For God so loved the world, that he gave
his one and only Son, that whoever ...

"Whoever" Means "Everyone"

One of the most amazing aspects of God's character is that he loves *all* people. *Everyone* is given the *opportunity* to be a part of God's family with the hope of eternal salvation.

This really includes *everyone*. It includes those who have never given their parents a lick of trouble, and it includes those who have worried their parents to the point of premature gray hair. This includes those who have risen to great heights and those who have not accomplished anything of which the world would take notice. This includes those who have been a part of God's church since infancy and who served as teacher, leader, or deacon, and it also includes those who have written graffiti on the walls of the church building and mocked those who tried to share their love for Christ. It includes those in prison and those who are part of a violent gang or the mafia. It includes terrorists, and those engaged in every other type of evil and vice. God's love and call applies to "all!" As such, God's invitation is to *all.*

> [12]Yet to *all* who received him, to those who believed
> in his name, he gave the right to become children of

God— [13]children born not of natural descent, nor of human decision or a husband's will, but born of God.[1]

Anyone who chooses to follow God can be born again in a spiritual renewal that makes him or her a new person. It doesn't matter what church denomination that person is from, or whether he or she even comes from a church background. It doesn't matter whether one comes from an honored people or a despised people. Race doesn't matter. Heritage doesn't matter.

[12]For there is no difference between Jew and Gentile— the same Lord is Lord of *all* and richly blesses all who call on him, [13]for, "Everyone who calls on the name of the Lord will be saved."[2]

God longs to have all people turn to him. He wants to save and care for *all* of his creation. God goes to extraordinary lengths to induce each of us to turn to him and choose to be a part of his family and to live according to his teaching and guidance. He longs for each of us to be his children. He doesn't want to loose any precious souls.

He is patient with you, not wanting anyone to perish, but *everyone* to come to repentance.[3]

What this all means is that no matter who we are, or what our past has been like, we have the opportunity to come to God and to obtain forgiveness of our sins, salvation, and the hope of eternal life with God. No one is too bad, too ugly, too lacking in talent, or too much of a mess. God wants us *all*.

---

[1] Jn.1:12.
[2] Ro.10:12-13.
[3] 2Pe.3:9.

Do We Really Have a Choice?

Some contend that God or DNA or some other factor has programmed us to be who we are and we can't change. Our English word, "sin," translates a Greek term meaning "missing the mark."[4] It was used in the ancient world for archers who missed the mark on the target. Paul describes, "sin" as "falling short" of God's glory.[5] We can't be guilty of missing the mark or falling short spiritually if we are exactly what God designed and programmed us to be without any way of being anything different. Our own biology and environment affect who we are to some degree. Sometimes we are so stuck in a lifestyle that we *feel* like we cannot change. But the concept of sin, so prevalent in the Bible, requires the ability of one to choose a course in life different than what God wants. It requires "free will," the ability to rise above one's own biology and environment and choose one's direction in life.

Sin is *all*-inclusive and therefore God's call goes out to *all*. All the great teachers of morality and all religious leaders sin. The Apostle Paul may have been the greatest missionary and Christian apologetic writer in the history of the world. And yet, he acknowledged his own struggle with sin.[6] With the single exception of Jesus, *all* fall short and miss the mark of what God wants, which is perfection.[7] Sin results in separation from God, or "spiritual death." All people sin and face spiritual death[8] and thus all people need Jesus to reconnect with God. God is not willing that *any* should perish.[9] That is why Christ died for *all*[10] and salvation is offered

---

4   *The New Strong's Expanded Dictionary of Bible Words*, by James Strong, Nashville, Thomas Nelson Publishers, 2001, §266 αμαρτια (*hamartia*), p.935.
5   Ro.3:23.
6   Ro.7:7-24.
7   Mt.5:48.
8   Ro.3:10, 21-23.
9   2Pe.3:9.
10   1Ti.2:6; 4:10; Heb.2:9; 2Pe.2:1; 1 Jn.2:2; 4:14.

to *all.*[11] Jesus told his followers to spread the Good News to *all* nations.[12] God wants *all* of us.

God calls on *all* people to repent.[13] "Repentance" requires a change of mind and direction.[14] It is turning to get back on God's intended course. God wouldn't need to call on us to repent to be and do what he wanted us to do, if we were simply programmed to act. He would simply pre-set our programming and there would be no need for a call to repent. The call is given to encourage *all* of us to choose God's way over our own.

And yet, there is an element of call, plan, and even predestination in the words of God. God has a plan. In the Old Testament God called out one tribal family (the descendants of Jacob) to be his people. These Hebrews, later called Jews, were set apart to show the world the difference between walking with God and walking without God. God wanted them to reach out to *all* people so that *all* could be God's people.[15] Unfortunately, they failed to reach out to non-Jews as God had intended and often failed to live up to the standards God taught them.

God then called *all* people through Jesus and commanded his disciples to share the good news of Jesus Christ with *all* people.[16] God knows the heart of man, knows what will happen before it occurs, and knows who will accept his call even before they do. Thus to some it may appear God pre-determines who will choose him.

---

[11] Ti.2:11; Jn.3:15f; 4:13f; 11:26; 12:46; Ac.2:21.

[12] Mt.28:19.

[13] Isa.31:6; Joel 2:13f; Mt.18:3; Acts 3:19; Mt.3:2; Lk.13:3-5; Acts 2:38; 17:30; Jn.6:29; Acts 16:31; 1 Jn.3:23.

[14] *Repentance.* Μετανοεω (*metanoeo*): "to think differently. ...Signifies (1) 'to change one's mind or purpose,' (1a) always, in the NT, involving a change for the better." *The New Strong's Expanded Dictionary of Bible Words*, by James Strong, Nashville, TN: Thomas Nelson Publishers, 2001, p.1233, §3340.

[15] Isa.42:6-7; 49:6; 49:22; 51:4; 58:6-8; 60:1-3. "Nations" (plural) = gentiles (non Jews).

[16] Mt.28:19.

But knowing ahead of time what will happen is not predetermining the choices another will make.

I think God's view of time and events is like he is looking at it on a great wall mural. He can look at any particular point in time because he is outside of time. Thus, if he chooses to do so, he can view Abraham and Sarah as they gave birth to Isaac, about year 2000 BC, or he can look at some event in the year AD 2025. He can view each event as if it was present to him. Sometimes he intervenes and shapes events, and other times he just lets it run. Thus knowing what will happen is not the same as making it happen.

What is predetermined is the change God has in store for those who choose to be lead by him. Those who accept the call and persevere in God's training are predetermined to be saved. They are entitled to all the benefits that come from being adopted into the family of God.[17] Those who commit themselves to God are predetermined to be changed little by little over a lifetime into the likeness of Christ. The *choice* is not predetermined. It is the *result* of one committing to God through Christ that is predetermined.

It's a bit like joining the Marines. The recruitment call is made to all citizens. Nobody is drafted into the Marines. One *chooses* to join the Marines. However, once one joins, commits to the training, and completes the training, he or she *will be* changed. Just talk to any Marine. It doesn't matter how many years have passed. Something is different about that Marine. The choice was not predetermined. But the change resulting from the commitment and training was.

Grace

In the last chapter, we looked at the way God's justice is carried out when someone pays the death sentence himself, or when a sinless person pays the spiritual sentence and debt for someone else as a

---

[17] Ro.8:28-29.

substitutionary sacrifice. When Jesus died on the cross, justice was thus served. The debt or sentence was paid in full. But there is also an inseparable role for grace in the heart of God both for our initial salvation and our ongoing need of forgiveness.

Our English word "grace" comes from a Greek term that describes the nature of a gift. Literally it means "thanks, benefit, gift, gracious, joy, liberality."[18] Grace is the attitude of giver upon bestowing a gift the recipient did not earn, or the thankfulness that flows from receiving an unearned gift.[19] It is often described as "unmerited favor." In contrast, something earned is called "compensation," not "grace."

God *gives* salvation to *all* who will commit to him. He *gave* Jesus to die on the cross so that *unworthy* people could be saved from spiritual death. God didn't send Jesus to die on the cross because we were so good that God was compelled to do so to pay us back for our goodness. God sent his son to die on the cross while we were completely undeserving.[20] Since salvation is a *gift*, and not earned by our goodness or works, we do not need to feel insecure about whether we are good enough. Nobody is too lost or too poor a candidate for God's family. God's grace is *not* dependent on *our* perfection or goodness. As such, it is available to *all* who will commit to him.

Salvation by faith and grace is a difficult concept since most of us expect to receive what we have earned. But the Christian message is that *if* we will choose to commit to Christ and depend on God through Jesus to guide us and save us, then God will take us, give us his Spirit to live within us, work with us, and help shape us little by little into the people he wants us to be. The key is not

---

[18] *Grace.* χαρις (*charis*): "Grace indicates favor on the part of the giver, thanks on the part of the receiver." *The New Strong's Expanded Dictionary of Bible Words,* by James Strong, Nashville, TN: Thomas Nelson Publishers, 2001, §5485, p.1451-1452.

[19] "It contains the idea of kindness which bestows upon one what he has not deserved." *Thayer's Greek-English Lexicon of the New Testament*, Peabody, MA: Hendrickson Publishers, Inc., 2012, §5485, p.666.

[20] Ro.5:8.

how good we are. We know we will fall short, in small and big ways, an uncountable number of times over a lifetime. But, as long as we keep coming back, and recommitting to God, and truly repenting of our sins, then God will stand by us, guide us in life, and take us by the hand to our eternal home with him in heaven. As long as we persevere and remain willing to be shaped and trained by God, he will continue to work with us and keep us as his.[21]

We don't wait until we are good enough to commit to God. We commit to God so that he can start shaping and helping us to become the people that we can only be with his help. Delay in making the commitment only delays the start of the changes that will make us who we can truly be.

Johnny Come Lately

Some feel it is unfair if he or she has been active in the Church for years, and others make their decisions for Christ late in life or on their deathbeds. Don't those who have worked all their lives serving the Lord deserve something better than those who choose at the last minute, after living a life of sin apart from God?

There are several factors to consider in answering the above questions. First, those who have served God for a lifetime have the benefit of knowing God throughout their lifetimes. These people have known how to live victorious spiritual lives all along. They have experienced the joy of serving others and God. They have had the confidence that they have been solidly in the arms of God with the hope of an eternity with God throughout their long years of service to God. They have been a part of the extended family of God throughout their walk with God. These are tremendous benefits in life that the person who chooses God at the *end* of his or her life has missed.

---

[21] Col.1:22-23; Heb.3:6.

Paul touched on the issue when asked if there was any advantage to being a lifetime Jew over the Gentiles. The Gentiles were just then being adopted into the family of God without having to become Jews first. Paul explained the Jews have "been entrusted with the very words of God."[22]

Jesus tells the story of a prodigal son that emphasizes the benefits of one who is always a part of God's family.[23] One son, contrary to his father's desire, takes his inheritance and squanders it with indulgent living. He runs out of money and lives a miserable life for a time a part from his father and family. Eventually he returns to his father begging for mercy and help. His father welcomes him and throws a feast. The other son, who has never waivered in his faithfulness, is indignant. Why should the prodigal son be honored? After all, it is the other son who remained true to the father throughout. The father explains the faithful son had always had the blessings of the family.

> [31]"'My son,' the father said, 'you are always with me, and everything I have is yours. [32]But we had to celebrate and be glad, because this brother of yours was dead and is alive again; he was lost and is found.'"[24]

So, yes, the person who serves God all throughout his or her life does obtain benefits and rewards that the deathbed Christian does not experience.

Second, when God adopts people into his family, he is not paying their wages or some *earned* compensation. He is shaping their hearts. It doesn't matter whether it takes a lifetime or a moment. The end result God desires is a soft heart that can be shaped by God. Jesus taught this lesson through a parable in which the owner of a vineyard paid the same wage to workers who came in to work

---

[22] Ro.3:1-2.
[23] Lk.15:11-32.
[24] Lk.15:31-32.

at different start times.[25] Some complained that was unfair. The owner emphasized that he gave each person what he promised to give and that he had the right to give the same wage to each person who came and worked in his field, regardless of when they arrived. In other words, the ultimate question is not *when* you commit to God, but *whether* you commit to God and permit him to shape your heart.

Even Me

I'm not a bad person. I compare favorably to most people. But next to Christ's never ending love, sacrificial giving, commitment to purity, dedication to God's mission, and unselfish spirit, I can see I have many failings. When the Bible says, "There is none righteous, no not one,"[26] God is talking about me.

As a High School student I was in the Varsity Club and participated in the behavior common to many of the people with whom I associated. We skipped school, teepeed houses of people we knew, egged houses and cars, dropped a pumpkin on a car, made fun of some people, and I went too far with some of the girls I dated. Following High School I had the freedom of a freshman in college with no parental supervision and no compelling Christian guidance to keep me from indulging in the selfishness that is typical of that age.

And yet, as my college indulgences grew, so did my introduction to Christ and his church. Doug was the first fellow Freshman I met at college. He was a Christian and he invited me to a church dinner during Orientation Week. Soon I was active in church beyond just Sunday morning. I was becoming more and more involved in the church and in Bible study.

---

[25] Mt.20:1-15.
[26] Ro.3:10.

And so my activity and attachment to the church was growing at the same time I was diving deeper into self-indulgent activities that were contrary to biblical teaching. It was like I was leading a double life with each track diverging and moving farther apart. Both sides were growing and expanding until I felt like I was going to explode. One night I drank too much and couldn't attend church the next morning because of a hangover. I think that may have been the event that sparked the light in my head. I realized how foolish it was to try to live two contrary lifestyles. I called the minister for that fateful meeting at the student center where I decided to put on Christ in baptism.

Even now, after being a Christian for decades, I have failings. Sometimes I say things I shouldn't say, think thoughts I shouldn't think, do things I shouldn't do. Other times I fail to speak words of hope, stand up for what is right, appreciate what I have been given, or praise my God. Sometimes I am utterly caught up in myself with little awareness of the needs of others or the desires of God. I'm better than some and worse than others.

The types of people who have committed to Christ and changed dramatically as a result often surprise me. John Newton was captain of an 18th century slave trade ship. In 1748, after a long harsh life, he found himself in a severe storm that almost destroyed his ship. It was at this time that he also found Jesus and began reading the Bible and learning what God wanted for his life. He eventually gave up the slave trade and became an abolitionist and a priest. In 1779 he published a hymnbook that included some songs Newton himself wrote. One of the Newton originals included in this collection was perhaps the greatest hymn of all - *Amazing Grace*.[27]

Nicky Cruz was born in a Theistic Satanist family in Puerto Rico. His parents abused him physically and mentally. He eventually became the leader of the Mau-Maus, a New York City gang. He claims he stabbed 16 people and was implicated in a murder. In

---

[27] *John Newton*, online at http://en.wikipedia.org/wiki/John_Newton.

1958, after a diligent repeated effort by a minister, Cruz made his decision for Christ and later became a preacher.[28]

One thing I have learned, which has become implanted within my soul, is the confidence that God loves *all* of us and will accept anyone willing to change and become a part of his family. He loves me in spite of my failings and imperfections. He wants me to *turn my life over to him* so that he can shape me little by little and take me to live with him in heaven. He loves those who are better than me and he loves those who are worse than me. God loves *all* of us, sent Jesus to die for *all* of us, and wants each of us to choose to live with him in his family.

Summary

"Whoever" means "everybody." We all have the chance to become a part of God's family with the hope of eternal life. This is a life that begins here on earth and culminates in God's heaven. All we need to do is commit to letting God lead. When we get off track, we repent, and get back on track. His grace will cover our failures.

Thought Questions

1. Do you ever feel unworthy of God's salvation? Why?

2. In light of our failures and shortcomings, how is it that God can want to save us and make us to be part of his family?

3. Why is it so easy to think that some people are too bad for God to consider saving?

---

[28] *Mau Maus*, online at http://en.wikipedia.org/wiki/Mau_Maus.

4. Why do we have a tendency to think newcomers to salvation don't deserve as much as those who have belonged to Lord all their lives?

5. What is your story for Christ? If you were raised in the church, what kind of benefits did you receive for spending a lifetime with Christ? If you came to Christ later in life, what was it like joining yourself to Christ?

9

Believes In Him

*For God so loved the world, that he gave his one
and only Son, that whoever believes in him ...*

Belief

The key to forgiveness of sin, salvation, and the hope of eternity with God, is an active belief in the God of the Bible. The word "belief" is a translation of the noun πιστις (*pistis*) meaning "conviction something is true," or "reliance on the conviction that something is true."[1] As a verb (πιστευω – *pisteuo*) the term refers to the action of trusting and depending on something or someone because of belief. This is commonly called "faith."

Christian "belief" (aka "faith") leads to action. Someone who truly believes relies on or trusts in the object of that belief enough to act on it. You probably won't climb a ladder unless you believe it will hold your weight. You won't let a surgeon operate on you unless you believe that surgeon has the necessary skill. Christian faith requires belief in who God is, in what Christ has done to save us, and in what his Spirit is doing to enable us to live the life we are called to live.[2]

---

[1] *The New Strong's Expanded Dictionary of Bible Words*, by James Strong, Nashville: Thomas Nelson Publishers, 2001, §4103, πιστις (*pistis*), "persuasion, i.e. credence, conviction,...reliance," p.1315.

[2] Heb.11:6.

If you truly believe that God exists, that he knows what is best for you, that he really does love you, and that he can offer you the truly abundant life, then you will listen to him, follow his direction, and do what he asks of you. Real belief means reading his words and searching for direction in the Bible. Real belief means trusting in God's leadership and strength. It means doing what God says to do.

There are times when someone believes in God *intellectually* and yet rejects God's leadership. This is open rebellion to God.[3] Those who believe in the existence of God and yet refuse to trust him, don't really believe he knows what is best, that he really does care for the believer, or that he can lead the believer into the abundant life. All they have is a belief in the existence, or some faulty view of the existence, of God. The biblical use of "belief" (πιστευω – *pisteuo*), in terms of salvation, always requires "trust" and "dependence" in God.

> [14]What good is it, my brothers, if a man claims to have faith but has no deeds? Can such faith save him? [15]Suppose a brother or sister is without clothes and daily food. [16]If one of you says to him, "Go, I wish you well; keep warm and well fed," but does nothing about his physical needs, what good is it? [17]In the same way, faith by itself, if it is not accompanied by action, is dead.[4]

Salvation

If we were able to live sinless lives, there would be no sins to separate us from God and there would be no need for the forgiveness that reconciles us to God through Christ. Unfortunately, because we are not able to live sinless lives, attempts to rely on our own ability

---

[3] Ja.2:19.
[4] Ja.2:14-17.

are misguided. It is pinning our hopes on what *we* can do. It is a *works* based approach to salvation. Because the passing grade is "perfection"[5] and we all fall short of God's ideal for us,[6] this approach will *not* result in salvation. It guarantees failure. We are called to perfection as defined and modeled by God himself. It is so easy to do what we shouldn't or to not do what we should. Either of these is missing the mark and falling short of God's ideal for us. Even the smallest of sins is a violation of God's law, separates us from God, and results in the sentence of judgment.[7] We simply can't be good enough to earn our own salvation.

The only viable approach to salvation is "faith" based. It is dependence on *God*, and therefore guarantees success. God will not let us down and thus our salvation is assured. We commit to cling to God and allow him to lead, guide and save us. When we slip off course, we repent and recommit to God's life. The passing grade comes not from how well I live my life, but from my trust in God as I commit to letting him save and change me.

Paul puts it this way. It is a choice between (1) an attempt to earn righteousness by what we do, or (2) accepting the righteousness that comes from God. Being a Jew, and having a great love for his own people, Paul sorrowfully wrote about those who would not turn to Christ for righteousness.

> [3]Since they did not know the righteousness that comes from God and sought to establish their own, they did not submit to God's righteousness. [4]Christ is the end of the law so that there may be righteousness for everyone who believes.[8]

---

5   Mt.5:48.
6   Ro.3:10; 21-23.
7   Ja.2:9.
8   Ro.10:3.

Faith doesn't typically come perfectly the day we commit to Christ. It grows with each step we take walking with God and trusting in his leadership. One day a man came to Jesus to ask for help. Jesus explained the importance of faith. The man responded, "I do believe; help me overcome my unbelief!"[9] This is a prayer we all need to pray because the lack of complete and perfect trust in the leadership of God in our lives shows that we all still have some "unbelief."

God's refusal to abandon us when we fail to measure up is called "grace," which we talked about in the last chapter. A good way to remember what it means is the acronym "<u>G</u>od's <u>R</u>iches <u>A</u>t <u>C</u>hrist's <u>E</u>xpense." All who die to themselves to be united with Christ and his sacrifice, are adopted by God and forgiven of their failures.

> [8]For it is by grace you have been saved, through faith—
> and this not from yourselves, it is the gift of God— [9]not
> by works, so that no one can boast.[10]

Shaping

Faith in God consists of turning our lives over to God so that he can help us reach our potential. It is sincerely saying to God, "Create in me a pure heart, O God, and renew a steadfast spirit within me."[11] It is asking God to make us something more than we can make of ourselves.

---

[9] Mk.9:24.

[10] *Through faith.* Eph.2:8-9. The contextual subject of this passage is salvation. The "gift" referenced here is that of salvation (i.e. "you have been saved"). Some mistakenly pick the word "faith" to be the referenced gift and presume that God is giving out faith as a gift. But faith is just the means by which the gift is given. It is clear from the passage that salvation is the gift referenced in this passage.

[11] Ps.51:10.

In the Olympic gymnastics, each little flaw, though imperceptible to most people, results in a score deduction. Even the greatest gymnasts do not typically achieve perfect scores. They miss the mark or fall short. Nadia Comăneci made history in 1976 as the first gymnasts to be awarded a perfect "10." To help the athlete reach his or her potential every gymnast has a coach. The coach helps the athlete see sloppiness, imperfect posture, or landings that aren't quite right. A coach helps the gymnast accomplish what the gymnast could not possibly accomplish alone. The coach encourages and demands that athlete reach for his or her potential. The coach shows the athlete how to reach victory.

God does this with all of his followers. Those who have faith – who trust in God's leadership – will listen to God, do what he asks, and seek with all his or her heart to be what God desires. Little by little we are changed into what God wants us to be. God takes our imperfections and gradually transforms and shapes them day by day towards perfection.

> And we, who with unveiled faces all reflect the Lord's glory, are being transformed into his likeness with everincreasing glory, which comes from the Lord, who is the Spirit.[12]

In the spiritual arena, Jesus Christ is the one and only one who has been awarded the perfect score.[13] He is the sole person described as "sinless." Jesus is God incarnate and God's nature is the definition of "sinless." Thus we seek to be like Christ.

That is not to say that we will look exactly like Jesus in personality and style any more than all gymnasts will look like Nadia in personality and style. It means rather that we seek the spiritual perfection that Jesus accomplished.

---

[12] 2Co.3:18.
[13] Isa.53:11; 2Co.5:21; Heb.4:15; 1Pe.2:22; 1 Jn.3:5.

Faith as a Journey

Walking by faith is somewhat like walking down a long road towards an end destination. As Christians, our end destination is God and his home – heaven [14] But it is not just about the destination. The journey itself is important. It is a journey on a spiritual road filled with the adventure of meeting new people and challenges. God brings us into contact with opportunities to serve and grow and be shaped into what God created us to be. It is on this road, walking with God, that we grow to know and appreciate God.

As we walk down the road to God's heaven, there are distractions on either side of the road. We may start looking at something off the road and drift off the road towards the focus of our eyes without even realizing it. Or we may see something we want to see or experience off the road and consciously turn off the road to explore this new adventure. In a spiritual sense, this is "sin" because it is wandering off the King's Highway – the road of righteousness. However, if we eventually realize we have wandered off the road and turn back to continue on down the King's Highway, then we have not truly abandoned God. In a spiritual sense, this turning back to the King's Highway is "repentance."

You could also think about faith living as flying an airplane. The pilot charts a perfect course. However, it is just about impossible for a pilot to keep the plane manually on target 100% of the time. The plane tends to meander a bit to and fro ("sin"). For the pilot, veering off course is not fatal as long as the pilot corrects. In fact, the pilot is constantly making small directional changes to bring the plane back on course. We do the same thing when driving a car. As long as one keeps making course corrections when he or she meanders off course, then the driver will reach the destination. Of course the farther the pilot or driver meanders off course, the more work it will take to get back on course.

---

[14] Col.3:1; Heb.3:1.

Walking by faith (or faith living) does not mean never getting off course. It means repeatedly turning back to get on course again. As long as we are repenting and turning back to God (making course corrections), we have not abandoned God and God will not abandon us. It is when we stop making corrections (fail to repent) that we are in danger of being permanently separated and lost to God.[15]

The only fatal sin is unrepented sin. This is described in the Old Testament as blatant repeated sin.[16] It is refusing to follow God's lead and refusing to repent and turn back to God. It is rebellion to God. In the New Testament it is called "blasphemy of the Holy Spirit," because it is rejection of the Holy Spirit, who is the last witness to our hearts of God's good news. It is the one sin for which there is no forgiveness.[17] Forgiveness is the process for overcoming the separation from God caused by sin. Forgiveness eliminates the barrier to uniting with and growing close to God. Spiritual forgiveness is meaningless to those who do not want to be with God or follow his way.

Faith as Repentance

Although repentance is primarily a changing of one's mind and direction, to return to the path God desires for our lives, there is an emotional element that is important for permanent change. That element is regret, sorrow, and a realization of how destructive and hurtful sin is. It is only when we *feel* the hurt that sin causes to God and others, and when we begin to understand its destruction, that we are truly motivated to avoid sin in the future.

The New Strong's Expanded Dictionary of Bible Words, *by James Strong,* explains that there are three steps to real and meaningful repentance. (1) There is "new knowledge" in which

---

[15] Ro.11:22; 1Co.9:27; Gal.5:4; Heb.2:1; Ja.5:19; Col.1:22-23; Heb.3:6.
[16] Nu.15:30-31; 1Jn.3:6.
[17] Mk.3:28-29.

one realizes or is made aware of the existence of the sin and its harmful consequences. (2) There is "regret" for the sinful action and "displeasure" with oneself for undertaking the action. (3) There is a real "change" of action or direction to get on God's track.[18]

"Repentance," without the emotional realization of the destructive hurtful nature of sin to God and others, will not last. One who makes light of his sin will never permanently turn away from that sin. We don't want to beat ourselves up each time we slip, because in so doing we cover ourselves with valueless self-inflicted emotional bruises. On the other hand, we do not want to underestimate the harmful effect of denying sin's destructive nature.

King David committed adultery, had Bathsheba's husband placed in a battle position to be killed, and then tried to cover up his sin.[19] When confronted with his sin he broke down, repented and wrote a beautiful Psalm expressing his sorrow, his understanding of the destructive nature of his sin, and his pleading to God for mercy and direction.

> Have mercy on me, O God, according to your unfailing love; according to your great compassion blot out my transgressions. Wash away all my iniquity and cleanse me from my sin. For I know my transgressions, and my sin is always before me. Against you, you only, have I sinned and done what is evil in your sight, so that you are proved right when you speak and justified when you judge. Surely I was sinful at birth, sinful from the time my mother conceived me. Surely you desire truth in the inner parts; you teach me wisdom in the inmost place. Cleanse me with hyssop, and I will be clean; wash me, and I will be whiter than snow. Let me hear joy and gladness;

---

[18] *The New Strong's Expanded Dictionary of Bible Words,* by James Strong, Nashville, TN: Thomas Nelson Publishers, 2001, p.1233, §3340 μετανοεω.

[19] 2Sa.11.

let the bones you have crushed rejoice. Hide your face from my sins and blot out all my iniquity. Create in me a pure heart, O God, and renew a steadfast spirit within me. Do not cast me from your presence or take your Holy Spirit from me. Restore to me the joy of your salvation and grant me a willing spirit, to sustain me. Then I will teach transgressors your ways, and sinners will turn back to you. Save me from bloodguilt, O God, the God who saves me, and my tongue will sing of your righteousness. O Lord, open my lips, and my mouth will declare your praise. You do not delight in sacrifice, or I would bring it; you do not take pleasure in burnt offerings. The sacrifices of God are a broken spirit; a broken and contrite heart, O God, you will not despise.[20]

God will not abandon a sinner who repents. This is what God wants in each of us. King David was called "a man after God's heart."[21] God wants us to recognize and acknowledge our sin, feel its destructive and harmful consequences, and turn back to God and commit to his teaching.

If we confess our sins, he is faithful and just and will forgive us our sins and purify us from all unrighteousness.[22]

"Confession" is an honest acknowledgement of the sin coupled with a deep realization of the nature of the sin and desire to turn away from the sin. This is real repentance, and God will forgive the sin of a penitent follower.

---

[20] Ps.51:1-17.

[21] Ac.13:21.

[22] 1Jn.1:9.

Faith as Dependence

There is a danger in claiming to be "Christian" without allowing God to lead. The term "Christian" itself means "follower of Christ."[23] Sometimes we simply use God as a convenient way to justify what we have already chosen to do on our own. Sometimes we begin with a presupposition that does not come from God and then seek ways of justifying our actions based on those erroneous presuppositions. We either re-translate Scripture or selectively quote Scripture out of context to support our presuppositions and life choices. Perhaps all of us do this in varying measure because we all struggle with our own biases. But to the degree that we try to bend Scripture to fit our own presuppositions and actions, we are acting contrary to the nature of faith.

Faith, or belief, is "dependence" on God and his instructions for life. It is an active, and not just an intellectual, assent.[24] Faith is allowing God to lead, change, and make me into the person he wants me to be – which is far more than I could ever be by myself. Our faith is evidenced by the degree to which we allow God to lead us in life. This faith will show in our actions.[25]

The Rope Walk

I have been to Hume Lake Christian Camp several times for Christian Education conferences. The camp is located in the Sequoia National Forest of Fresno County, California. It is a beautiful setting in the mountains on the edge of a lake.

---

[23] *Christian.* "Follower of Christ," *The New Strong's Expanded Dictionary of Bible Words,* by James Strong, Nashville, TN: Thomas Nelson Publishers, 2001, §5546 χριστιανος, p.1458.

[24] Ja.2:19.

[25] Ja.2:14-26.

Years ago I signed up for my first ropewalk at one of those conferences. A ropewalk is a series of ropes, stretched from tree to tree, high above the ground. There is a rope upon which a participant walks like a tightrope walker with some additional ropes overhead for holding and lifelines. I always get a little nervous with heights and this time was no exception. I was about to try something I had never done before at a height that would cause many to tremble.

I slowly climbed up the rope ladder that clung to the trunk of a tree. At the top of the ladder stood a small platform with a worker who clipped me to a lifeline that would follow overhead as I walked across the rope course. Being clipped to the lifeline I couldn't fall very far, and yet my heart was still pounding as I took the first step off the platform and onto the rope deathly high above the ground. Slowly but surely I worked my way across that first rope only to find at the next platform there was another rope to walk.

Then I got stuck. The woman in front of me panicked and froze. She didn't believe she could take another step and needed help. I watched as the worker at the next platform talked with her, encouraged her, and tried to help her understand that she could move forward and finish the walk. He reminded her that she was hooked to a lifeline and therefore could not fall. He explained that many had taken this path before. Some had also panicked, but that they had all completed the journey. He let her know that he believed she too could achieve this victory. She just needed to trust him and the lifeline to which she was hooked. Then she could move forward and take the journey one step at a time. The woman started slowly moving again and eventually finished the entire course.

On the ground we talked about what had happened to all of us. We discussed how we sometimes conclude that we cannot go on when faced with a challenge that takes us way out of our comfort zone. We also talked about how all the trivial things in our lives were forgotten as we focused on the immediate challenge. In reality it all came down to faith. We had to have faith in the course itself, the lifeline, and in the workers who were guiding us through the course. Then we could move forward, one step at a time.

The challenges we face in life can be much more significant than making it through a rope course which gives us a few moments of fear. But the principle for making it through the really tough challenges is the same. Walking the Christian life in a world filled with selfishness, unfairness, suffering and danger is tough. Facing illness, economic woes, and other challenges can be daunting and frightening at times. But God has promised that if we *trust* him, and if we follow his lead, we will make it through successfully. We simply need to trust, and then move forward one step at a time.

Summary

The key to salvation in Christ is "faith." Faith is belief, trust, and dependence on God's leadership through the actions of Jesus. We will never be good enough to earn our salvation. Thus we are compelled to choose the other option - salvation by faith through grace in what Jesus did on the cross.

Thought Questions

1. What does "faith" mean to you?

2. What is the difference between trying to earn your salvation by your works and good deeds, and achieving salvation through faith in what God has done through Jesus Christ?

3. How does "faith" help shape us into what we can and should be?

4. What role does "repentance" play in a faith based approach to salvation?

5. When have you had to depend on something or someone? How did that experience illustrate the nature of faith in spiritual salvation?

10

Shall Not Perish

For God so loved the world, that he
gave his one and only Son, that whoever
believes in him shall not perish ...

The Nature of Sin

The Bible says, "God is light; in him there is no darkness at all."[1]
God is absolutely pure and holy and will not permit sin in his home.

This is trouble, because none of us is without sin. Which of us
has never said something to hurt another? Which of us has never
acted selfishly? Which of us has always taken the opportunities
afforded us to do good for others? Which of us has always taken the
opportunities afforded to us to share the good news of Jesus Christ?

The Bible answers the questions above with a resounding
"none." Except for Jesus,[2] there are none who are righteous or
right before God by their own strength and doing.[3] All fall short of
the glory of God.[4] Anyone who says he is without sin is deceiving
himself.[5] We may appear to be "righteous" when compared with

---

[1]   1Jn.1:5.
[2]   Heb.4:15.
[3]   Ro.3:10.
[4]   Ro.3:23.
[5]   1Jn.1:8.

other sinners. But when we compare ourselves to divine perfection, we don't look quite as good. We are all sinners.

The Bible is full of examples of sin. Sin is despising one's neighbor.[6] It is knowing to do good and not doing it.[7] It is deceiving others.[8] It is disobedience, allowing ourselves to be enslaved by all kinds of passions and pleasures, and a lifestyle of malice, envy and hatred.[9] It is squandering one's wealth and wild living.[10] It is being quarrelsome and engaging in gossip.[11] It is divorce.[12] It is murder.[13] It is misusing the name of the Lord.[14] It is failing to honor one's father or mother.[15] It is committing adultery.[16] It is stealing.[17] It is coveting what belongs to other people.[18] It is sexual immorality, impurity and debauchery, idolatry and witchcraft, hatred, discord, jealousy, fits of rage, selfish ambition, dissensions, factions and envy, drunkenness, orgies and the like.[19] Even a hint of sexual immorality is contrary to the will of God.[20] It is obscenity, foolish talk, and coarse joking.[21] It is sin to pick at the imperfections of someone else when you have problems in your own life.[22] It is even wrongful thinking and attitudes. [23]There are an infinite number of ways in which we can fall short of God's

---

6   Pr.14:21.
7   Ja.4:17.
8   2Ti.3:13.
9   Tit.3:3.
10 Lk.15:13.
11 Pr.26:21-22.
12 Mal.2:16.
13 Ge.4:8-12; Ex.20:13.
14 Ex.20:7.
15 Ex.20:12.
16 Ex.20:14.
17 Ex.20:15.
18 Ex.20:17.
19 Gal.5:19-21; Ja.3:16; 1Co.6:18.
20 Eph.5:3.
21 Eph.5:4.
22 Mt.7:3-5.
23 *Wrongful attitudes.* Selfish anger - Mt.5:22; Lust - Mt.5:28; Hate – Mt.5:44.

glorious ideal and the perfection to which he calls us.[24] Remember, "sin" is missing the mark and falling short of what God wants.

Sin, regardless of the type, has a tendency to create conflict within our own lives. Most of us know right from wrong and the way we should live. Failure to measure up to that standard typically creates grief, shame, frustration, anger and depression. The person who wants to do right and repeatedly falls, struggles with the contradiction. Even the great Apostle Paul faced the frustration of sin while wanting to be godly.[25] We should never underestimate the pain, grief, shame, and struggle one might have with sin.

Sin Hurts

Sin hurts others when we are negligent or cruel to them. It hurts us in that it makes it more difficult to get back on the course of faith living and eats away at our commitment to God. Sometimes sin even has destructive physical consequences in our lives. But most of all, sin hurts God.

God loves us, wants what is best for us, and has dreams for us. God feels the hurt when our sin hurts others. He is saddened when we sin in ways that hurt our own physical bodies or our spirituality. Just as a parent hurts inside when a child is disobedient, disrespectful, or undertakes a destructive lifestyle, God hurts when we sin. We should view sin as hurting not only ourselves and

---

[24] *Same sex sexual relationships are traditionally viewed as sin.* The traditional view is based on passages like Ge.1:27; 2:21-24; Mt.19:4-6; Eph.5:31; Lev.18:22-29; 20:13; Ro.1:26-27; 1Co.6:9-10; 1Ti.1:9-11. Some counter the traditional view with (1) the biblical passages should not be viewed as describing the *only* acceptable sexual behavior, (2) these passages do not apply today, (3) the translators have made errors in translation, (4) gay relationships can be inferred from interaction between people like David & Jonathan and Ruth & Naomi.

[25] Rom.7:7-24.

other people – but also God.[26] Too often we forget about or don't appreciate how our sin hurts God.

Sin has consequences in life here and now. Sin hurts now! Sin destroys trust between people. Sins of dishonesty and sexual promiscuity can destroy relationships. The sin of selfishness causes us to miss opportunities to provide meaningful service to others – the one immutable action that brings purpose of life. Sin destroys hope and can lead to depression. Sin breaks the relationship with God and cuts off the ability to hear the call of God.[27] People lost to sin are in the process of "perishing" *now*.

The Eternal Consequence of Sin

Yet there is a more serious eternal consequence of sin. The pure and holy God of the Bible cannot abide by sin. Sin results in separation from God.[28] This separation has been described as a wall and as a vast canyon. We face physical death at some point and, more seriously, we face spiritual death when we are alienated from God. Death is the consequence of sin.[29]

Almost all of us have family rules for our own homes, which set a certain tone for our families. These rules are an extension of our own personality and values. Certain conduct is not permissible in our homes. People who want to violate the moral tone of our homes are not invited in. Those who choose not to live by our house rules may live a life contrary to the tone of our homes elsewhere, but not in our homes. Those who don't like our rules, won't like being in our homes. More than likely, they won't like us.

If our children have been playing outside and come in filthy or muddy from head to toe, the first things we do is demand that

---

[26] Ge.39:9; Ex.32:33; 2Sa.12:13; 1 Ki.8:46.
[27] Isa.59:2.
[28] Isa.59:2.
[29] Ro.6:23.

they put their dirty clothes in some safe spot and then immediately shower or bathe. We are not about to let them tromp dirt or mud through the house. We have standards for our homes and most of us are not willing to allow mud and dirt to be freely spread around our home.

Heaven is the dwelling place of God.[30] God too has standards or "house rules" for his home to set the tone for heaven. God will not tolerate spiritual darkness in his home.[31] He desires to maintain a spiritually pure home. This is not just a decision made by God for his own preference. It arises out of the very nature of a God in whom there is no darkness. Thus only those committed to God and his sinless nature are permitted to reside in heaven. They are not sinless on this earth, but repentance and contrition follow their sin. They are penitent. They want to be with God and have accepted his invitation to live with him under *his* house rules. The blood of Jesus figuratively washes them before entering God's home – meaning they have accepted Christ's death on the cross as a substitutionary sacrifice for their sins. Only those washed clean of their sin by the blood of Jesus may enter God's home.

Those with active faith who lived prior to the death of Jesus, who did not know about Jesus, were also saved by the blood of Jesus and invited to God's home. Although obedience to God was required, Romans 3:25 indicates that sins were not fully addressed prior to the death of Jesus. Animal sacrifices had been established to teach people the need for sacrifice, but it was Jesus' sacrifice that really brought about salvation. In Romans 4 Paul explains that people like Abraham, who lived long before Christ's death on the cross, were saved by their faith. Abraham's trust in God was deemed the equivalent of a Christian's faith today because he was depending on God's leadership in his life. The blood of Jesus

---

[30] Dt.26:15; 1Ki.8:30; 2Ch.30:27; Job.22:12; Ps.73:25; 123:1; Isa.66:1; Lk.11:2; Ac.7:49.
[31] Rev.21:27.

covered those who truly had faith and depended on God prior to the historical death of Jesus on the cross.[32]

The Bible speaks of another place outside of heaven. Γεεννα (*gehenna*) is the Greek term we most often translate "hell."[33] Jesus speaks of "hell" as a place associated with the death of both body and soul.[34] It is something to avoid even if that avoidance means making huge sacrifices.[35]

Αδης (*hades*) is another Greek term we associate with "hell" that literally refers to the depths of the earth.[36] It is like the old Hebrew term הואש (*sheol*).[37] It includes the depths of the ground and the depths of the sea.[38] This makes sense. When people die, their bodies are most commonly buried in the ground, sent to the bottom of the sea, or they are cremated with ashes scattered on the ground. These are the places of the dead. Earth's depths are pictured as a spiritual prison for the dead. Jesus holds the key

---

[32] *People who don't know about Jesus.* The Bible does not clearly address the status of those who lived without knowledge of the Old Testament Law or the death, burial and resurrection of Jesus. All people have a basic knowledge of God (Rom.1:19) and thus trusting faith is possible in all. Romans 10:10-15 describes the need to preach the Good News of Jesus to all and rhetorically asks how one can call on the name of the Lord to be saved without being told about Jesus. Yet Luke 12:47-48 indicates that we are only held responsible for what we know and to the degree we know it. Our uncertainty on the status of those who never hear of Jesus does not affect the way we ourselves live our lives. We know, as people who are aware of Jesus, that (1) *we* need to trust in God through Jesus and (2) that God has called us to share his Good News of Jesus so that others may be blessed with the full abundant life.

[33] *The New Strong's Expanded Dictionary of Bible Words*, by James Strong, Nashville: Thomas Nelson Publishers, 2001, §1067 γεεννα (*geenna*) p.1021.

[34] Mt.10:28.

[35] Mk.9:43-48.

[36] *The New Strong's Expanded Dictionary of Bible Words*, by James Strong, Nashville: Thomas Nelson Publishers, 2001, §86, αδης (*hades*) p.914.

[37] *The New Strong's Expanded Dictionary of Bible Words*, by James Strong, Nashville: Thomas Nelson Publishers, 2001, §7585 הואש (*shehole*) p.828.

[38] Rev.20:13.

to this prison.[39] Those who do not choose Jesus face "the second death."[40] This "second death" is the eternal spiritual separation from God.

Because of sin, our default destination is hell. We face separation from God and are not invited into God's home. People who are separated from God and without God's renewing power, are described as "perishing."[41] The consequences of living without God will be – "hell." Without him, the goodness of life will be gone.

Some people think it is unfair that God only welcomes to heaven those who affirmatively choose him and his lifetsyle in heaven. But why would anyone who doesn't like God or his standard of living here on earth, want to spend eternity with that same God in heaven under God's house rules? During their lives on earth God works to convince people to desire life with him and to see the beauty of the pure life to which we are called. But God upholds the decisions of those who choose not to be with him. He will not force someone to live eternally with him when that person doesn't want to.

Confidence We Won't Perish

Because of what Jesus has done on the cross, people who trust and depend on God can have confidence they will not perish. They have chosen to live with God in all of his goodness under his house rules. Those who have chosen God through faith, will not be turned away. Rather, God adopts them as part of his family and invites them to live in his home.

As we have already discussed, grace is the means by which God gifts forgiveness and the abundant spiritual life to us *if* we will only trust and depend on him. We obtain the salvation we could never

---

[39] Rev.1:18.
[40] Rev.20:14-15.
[41] Lk.13:1-5; Jn.10:28; Ac.8:20; Ro.2:12; 2Thes.2:10; 2Pe.2:12.

earn. Instead of relying on our own abilities, we are relying on what God has done and is continuing to do. God will not fail us.

Even ongoing sin of the *penitent* sinner will not block that person from God. We know that we will still struggle with sin throughout our physical lives. But the sinner who repents, regardless of how many times repentance is required, can be confident that God will welcome him or her to his home in heaven.[42] Remember, God's purpose is to shape us, not judge us.

It is the commitment to God and his leading that brings this confidence. The question becomes, "Do I let God lead? Do I seek out God's direction in my life? When I am awakened to the fact that I have strayed from God's way, do I repent and get back on course?" If the answer to these questions is "yes," then one can have confidence in God's desire and ability to accomplish salvation. John wanted Christians to know that they would not perish.

> [13]I write these things to you who believe in the name of the Son of God so that you may know that you have eternal life.[43]

A Class Experience

Most of us have spent years in school as young people. I have spent about as much time as a student in formal education as anybody. I know the routine. Teacher gives assignments that are completed by the students and graded on their merits by the teacher. Tests, reports and writing assignments are graded by the quality of the work done. We *earn* the grade we get by the quality of our work. You never know what you will get as a grade until all the work is done and the grades are posted.

---

[42] 1Jn.1:9.
[43] 1Jn.5:13.

As an undergrad student myself, I once had an unusual English literature class that took a completely different approach to grading. It was spring of my freshman year. At the start of our first class, the professor said, "We are not going to have grades in this class." That got my attention. "I will give you assignments. You will read, write papers and engage in class discussion. I will make comments on your papers, but I will not give you a grade. On the last day of class I will ask you to take out a piece of paper, write your name on it, and also include the grade you would like to receive. I'll give you that grade for this class." That sounded pretty good to me! All I had to do was put what I wanted on a piece of paper and I would receive that grade? I concluded this was going to be an easy class.

I came to the next class, *not* having read the assignment. After all it didn't really matter since I didn't have to earn my grade. The first thing the professor asked was, "How many of you read the assignment?" About five hands went up out of a class of 30. "Those of you who did not read the assignment are dismissed from class." I was shocked. The professor kicked 25 of us out of class that day.

There was something about the professor and this strange class that made me want to come back. However, I realized I could only come back if I read the assignments. So I never missed another assignment. I worked hard in that class. As it turned out, it wasn't the easy class I had expected.

On the last day of class, true to his word, the professor said, "Please take out a piece of paper, write your name on it, and list the grade you should get in this class." I wrote a "B" thinking that was probably what I deserved. When I eventually saw my grades, I discovered the professor had given me an "A."

In thinking about this class it hit me that the professor did not want me to work for a grade. He wanted me to work for a higher purpose – that of learning and understanding. He wanted to transform me into a devoted student who would learn and mature for reasons other than simply to acquire a grade. As such he gave us the promise of the grade up front to let us know we would not be working to earn a grade. We already had the promise of the grade at the beginning of the first class. I already had the grade I wanted. My work was motivated by something else. It was motivated by the nature of the professor and the way he changed the way I looked at the class.

God works in similar fashion. He knows that none of us can get 100% or the A+ in life. No one is good enough to earn a passing grade for salvation and heaven. We just aren't that dedicated or that skilled. And so there is "grace." In essence God says, "You want the passing grade for heaven? Okay you've got it. Now that you know you have the grade you want, let's get down to work, not to earn your salvation or heaven, but rather to grow, learn, and mature for its own sake. Come get to know me and we will discover amazing things."

There is a particular attitude and conduct God wants in his classroom of life. He wants us to commit to him and to give the work our best effort.[44] If we don't try to do the assignments or engage in class, even after initially committing to the class, we will fail.[45] But if we persevere, put in the effort and participate in the work, two things will happen. (1) We will grow, mature and become spiritually stronger. (2) We will have our passing grade for salvation and heaven based on what *God has done* through grace, rather than on how good we are ourselves.[46]

---

[44] Col.3:23.

[45] *Failing.* "Those who fell"(Romans 11:22); "disqualified for the prize" (1 Corinthians 9:27); "fallen away from grace" (Galatians 5:4); "drift away"" (Hebrews 2:1); If we deliberately keep on sinning after we have received the knowledge of the truth, no sacrifice for sins is left" (Hebrews 10:26); wander from the truth (James 5:19); "if they fall away" (Hebrews 6:4); "again entangled in it and overcome, they are worse off at the end than they were at the beginning" (2 Peter 2:20).

[46] *Perseverance. If* you continue in your faith (Colossians 1:22-23); *if* we hold on to our courage and the hope of which we boast (Hebrews 3:6); *continue* in his kindness" (Romans 11:22).

Summary

Those who refuse to choose God perish. The Good News is that those who commit to God through Christ will *not* perish. Rather they will be adopted as God's children, discover the abundant life, and be welcomed into God's heavenly home.

Thought Questions

1. What does it mean to say, "God is light; in him there is no darkness at all?"

2. Is it helpful for you to think about sin as "missing the mark" or "falling short" of God's expectation? Why or why not?

3. Who all is hurt by sin?

4. What are the consequences of sin?

5. Why is God's grace so amazing?

11

But Have Everlasting Life

For God so loved the world, that he gave his
one and only Son, that whoever believes in
him shall not perish but have everlasting life.

Here is one of the key promises of the message of God. The one who chooses God through Christ has the hope of an everlasting life. There are two aspects of "eternal life" that make it truly important to each of us: length and quality.

The Length of Existence

First, eternal life deals with the *length* of existence. The eternal life promised by Jesus, begins immediately upon our conversion and commitment to Christ.

> "I tell you the truth, whoever hears my word and believes him who sent me *has* eternal life and will not be condemned; he *has* crossed over from death to life."[1]

Notice this passage refers to eternal life as *already in existence* for those who have have chosen Christ by faith. The first chapter in this

---

[1]   Jn.5:24.

eternal life will be the life we live in these physical bodies until the Lord calls us home to heaven.

The traditional viewpoint is that all people have an existence that lasts forever. Human life is eternal.[2] Our spiritual lives continue on beyond the death of our present physical bodies.[3] God views even the physically dead, as alive,[4] because spiritual souls do not die when the physical life ends. The physical body may die, and the soul may fall asleep for a time, but when judgment comes that soul will awaken to a new existence. People tend to sense that life does not end with the death of the physical body.[5] The prophet Daniel points out some of the dead will awake to "everlasting life," and others "to shame and everlasting contempt."[6] Jesus says the choice is between "everlasting punishment" and "everlasting life."[7] Jesus also said at the end the dead will rise and "those who have done good will rise to live, and those who have done evil will rise to be condemned."[8]

In contrast, some believe that only God's followers share an eternal existence. Proponents of this view contend that the lives of those who do not choose God are extinguished permanently at or just after the point of physical death and the sentence of judgment. This viewpoint has the challenge of trying to explain how biblical phrases like "everlasting contempt,"[9] "eternal fire,"[10] "eternal punishment,"[11] and the "fire that never goes out,"[12] do *not* infer everlasting existence. Typically this view relies on a rather technical

---

[2] Mt.25:46; Jn.6:27; 10:28; Ro.2:7; 6:22; 1Ti.6:19; Tit.1:2; 1 Jn.2:25; Jude 2.

[3] 1Co.15:42-44.

[4] Lk.20:38.

[5] Ecc.3:11.

[6] Da.12:2.

[7] Mt.25:46.

[8] Jn.5:29.

[9] Da.12:2.

[10] Mt.25:41.

[11] Mt.25:46.

[12] Mk.9:43.

approach. The claim is made that the *sentence* of death is *eternal*, but the spiritual *life* of the one sentenced *terminates* at judgment.[13]

The question is not whether there will be eternal consequences to our physical life choices, but rather what will our life choices lead to? Will it be eternal shame, punishment and condemnation, or will it be eternal life?

The Quality of Life

Secondly, "eternal life" deals with the *quality* of life. "Life" here refers to the *abundant* life of God and not merely existence. Jesus said,

> [10]The thief comes only to steal and kill and destroy; I have come that they may have life, and have it to the full.[14]

This life comes from God. It arises out of the joy of knowing God.[15] Paul, who had accomplished so much in his life, thought all that utterly worthless next to the wonder and joy of knowing Christ Jesus.[16]

The full abundant life comes as a result of living the life God calls us to live. Certain character traits tend to develop as we commit ourselves to God and allow his Spirit to fill and direct us. The abundant life is filled with purpose, meaning, and value – all of which come from God. It is a life characterized by the joy of knowing God and serving him, by contentment with what one has, and by selfless giving. What gradually fades away is the selfishness, jealousy, hatred, and bitterness that can otherwise consume us.

---

[13] *Hell A Final Word*, by Edward William Fudge, Abilene, TX: Leafwood Publishers, 2012.

[14] Jn.10:10.

[15] Jn.17:3.

[16] Php.3:7-10.

The abundant life here on earth is not a life void of any trouble. Biology and circumstances beyond our control often bring devastating storms and challenges into our lives. Sometimes our own actions bring trouble in our lives. Rather, the Christian life is an attitude and strength to help us deal with the challenges of life.[17]

Our ability to recognize the abundant life and live it depends on our willingness to allow God to lead and for his Spirit to control our attitudes and actions. Thus to the degree we allow sin to control our lives, we also block the joy and power of the abundant life promised by God.

The Holy Spirit

The gifting of God's Holy Spirit to dwell within each believer is an important part of the abundant everlasting life. God promises the gift of the Holy Spirit to all who commit to him.[18] The Holy Spirit dwells within each believer.[19] The Bible calls our bodies "the temple of the Holy Spirit."[20]

The Holy Spirit is the third person of the Trinity. The Spirit is a part of the very essence of God.[21] Personal pronouns and attributes are used for the Holy Spirit, implying a personal being.[22] Jesus

---

[17] 2Pe.1:5-8.

[18] Ac.2:38-39.

[19] Ro.8:9.

[20] 1Co.6:19.

[21] *Spirit.* The terms translated "Spirit" are Hebrew = חוּר (*ruach*) & Greek = πνευμα (*pneuma*). General definition: "breath, wind, breeze, spirit". Biblical absolute usage: "the mind, energy & life of God"

[22] *Personal pronouns.* Jn.14:26; 26:13-14. *Attributes.* Intellect (1Co.2:11); Sensibilities (Ro.8:27; 15:30); Will (1Co.12:11); Teaches (Lk.12:12; Jn.14:26; 1Co.2:13; 1Jn.2:27); Bears witness (Jn.15:26; Ro.8:16; Gal.4:6; 1Jn.3:24; 1Jn.4:13; 5:6); Convicts (Jn.16:8-11); Guides (Jn.16:13); Glorifies Christ (Jn.16:14); Calls people into service (Ac.13:2); Speaks (Ac.13:2; Rev.2:7); Directs (Ac.16:6f); Intercedes (Ro.8:26); Searches out (1Co.2:10).

promised the Holy Spirit in preparation for his departure from this physical earth. The permanent indwelling Spirit was not given until after the resurrection of Jesus.[23] Although God's Spirit worked in the Old Testament by *temporarily lighting* on individuals, God's Spirit now *resides permanently* within each believer committed to Christ.[24] Whereas long ago God's glory had filled the Tabernacle[25] (the special tent meeting place of God's people[26]), our own bodies *now* become the "temple of the Holy Spirit.[27]

God's Holy Spirit guides Christians into truth.[28] This is the part of God that meshes with our own physical bodies and mind to help us view life through God's eyes.[29] This Spirit helps us desire what God wants.[30] This Spirit helps us overcome our weakness and helps us in our prayer life.[31] This is the part of God living within us to help with the gradual change within our own hearts to think as God thinks.

> [22]The fruit of the Spirit is love, joy, peace, patience, kindness, goodness, faithfulness, [23]gentleness and selfcontrol. Against such things there is no law. [24]Those who belong to Christ Jesus have crucified the sinful nature with its passions and desires. [25]Since we live by the Spirit, let us keep in step with the Spirit.[32]

---

[23] Jn.7:39.
[24] Jn.14:17; Ro.8:9; 1Co.3:16.
[25] Ex.40:34-38.
[26] Ex.33:7-10.
[27] 1Co.3:16, 6:19.
[28] Jn.16:7-15.
[29] 1 Co.2:6-16.
[30] Ro.8:5-6.
[31] Ro.8:26-27.
[32] Gal.5:22-25.

Church Life

Church is an important part of the abundant life promised by Jesus. It is the joining of people together devoted to God's purposes. It is one of God's tools to shape us into people with loving hearts of service and to empower us to live this full promised life.

Although Christ's "church" and the "Kingdom of God" overlap in meaning and time, they are different. The Kingdom includes *all* people who have placed themselves in subjection to the divine King, from the beginning of the existence of people, during the here and now, and through all eternity. The church refers to one segment or time period of the Kingdom of God. Thus the church is a subset of the Kingdom. The church is made up of Kingdom People.

The "church" is the community of Christians that serves as the mouth, hands, and feet of God here on earth. Some call it, "God with skin." Jesus was crucified, raised and then ascended to the Father in heaven about AD 29-30. It was shortly after this ascension that his disciples were infused with the outpouring of the Holy Spirit described in the Bible at Acts 2. We call this outpouring the beginning of the church. It grew out of the synagogue, but took on a new dynamic with the infusion of the Holy Spirit and the focus on Jesus Christ. The church continues until physical life on earth ends.

Although there is a *universal church* that includes all Christians in all parts of the world, most commonly the term we translate "church" is used in the New Testament to refer to a *local congregation* of Christians working within a particular local community. An individual church is often identified in the Bible in connection with the town in which it is located.

The term "church" typically translates the ancient Greek term εκκλεσια (*ekklesia*), which means "a group of people called out to assemble together for a special purpose." It "was used among the Greeks of a body of citizens 'gathered' to discuss the affairs of state." It was commonly used of "a popular meeting."[33] In most cases when the term is used, it is joined by another modifying term to identify what type of assembly was being referenced. However, as the term became more and more associated with the Christian assembly, people began using the term in an absolute sense, without an additional modifier. It was just "the Assembly."[34] *Ekklesia,* aka "church," in the Christian sense refers to "those who assemble together to carry out the purposes of God through Jesus Christ." This basic meaning of the term tells us something crucial about the nature of the "church." It is a group thing. Christians are not meant to function alone. They are to work together with the support of a team.

It is important to note that the biblical use of the term "church" never refers to a physical building. There were no buildings constructed as church buildings in the first century when the New Testament was written. The term always refers to the assembly of people. Such assemblies can take place in a building, in an arena, in a house, or out in the open where there is no man made structure at all. It is the people, not the building, which is the "church" in the biblical sense.

The church is described collectively with many pictures in the Bible. It is the body of Christ,[35] illustrating how each of us plays a part as the hands, feet, eyes, and mouth of Christ. It is a *spiritual* building,[36] illustrating how we serve as shelter for those in need, protecting them from hostile elements of the world. It is the assembly (church) of Christ,[37] and the assembly (church) of God,[38]

---

[33] *The New Strong's Expanded Dictionary of Bible Words,* by James Strong, Nashville: Thomas Nelson Publishers, §1577 εκκλεσια, p.1068. See Ac.19:32-41 which uses the term for a secular municipal meeting.

[34] Mt.16:18; Ac.20:28; Eph.5:23; Col.1:18.

[35] Rom.12:5; 1Co.12:27; Eph.1:23.

[36] 1Co.3:9-10; Eph.2:21.

[37] Rom.16:16.

[38] 1Co.1:2.

illustrating how Christians *meet* together. It is a flock,[39] illustrating how we follow a shepherd (Jesus) wherever he leads. It is the bride of Christ,[40] illustrating the lifetime commitment we make to Christ. It is the household of God,[41] illustrating the family nature of the Christian community. It is the temple of God,[42] illustrating the spiritual purpose of the community of God.

Purpose and Mission

The people of God's Kingdom have a mission as part of the promised abundant life. One of the best descriptions of the nature and calling of God's people is found in the writings of Peter.

> You are a chosen people, a royal priesthood, a holy nation, a people belonging to God, *that you may* declare the praises of him who called you out of darkness into his wonderful light.[43]

Becoming a part of the family and Kingdom of God means taking on the responsibility of fulfilling the important work to which God has called us. Although there is a great deal of socializing within the church, the church is much more than a social club.

The Bible pictures life as a battle with the forces of evil.[44] Evil forces show themselves in a number of ways. There is cruelty, selfishness, pride, greed, and idolatry, all of which attack the wellbeing and health of God's greatest creation. These evil forces harm the people God loves.

---

[39] Ac.20:28-29; 1Pe.5:2.
[40] 2Co.11:2.
[41] 1Ti.3:15.
[42] 1Co.3:16.
[43] 1Pe.2:9.
[44] Eph.6:12.

The church is God's earthly team charged with the task of holding off these evil forces. Our defense plan is really a plan of offense with six prongs of attack. Although some are gifted to lead in one or more of these prongs, we should *all* be working on *all* six of these prongs at some level. The church is...

To Glorify God. God teaches that Christians should live a life that reflects the glory of God so that all may see and praise God.[45] We should talk the talk and walk the walk that helps people see God.[46] This is not simply a divine selfish desire for admiration. Rather, it is an attempt to lead people to (1) look to God for guidance to live life to the full, and (2) to see that God is the best thing there is in life. It is hoped that upon this realization, the person will commit to God through Christ, live God's life, thrive and be brought into the eternal family of God with the hope of heaven.

To Edify Itself. God teaches that church members should build one another up to grow the effectiveness of the church and the strength of each member.[47] Life is tough. Loss, illness, unemployment, persecution and depression can be devastating. God's family is a working team to encourage each other. Each person is gifted in a unique way to play an important role in carrying out this dynamic work. When each person fulfills his or her own role, the team works and the church grows healthy and strong. As a result each individual member is better able to live the victorious life even in the face of severe tests and hardships.

To Purify Itself. God through Christ is the one who truly purifies the church.[48] However, God teaches that the church is to help maintain pure living in its members and encourage course corrections when needed to grow and preserve that purity.[49] God is working to make us in to the people we should be. He is working

---

[45] 1Pe.2:9; 4:11.

[46] Mt.5:16; Jn.15:8.

[47] Eph.4:11-16; Ro.14:19; Eph.5:2.

[48] Eph.5:25-27.

[49] Eph.5:11; 1Ti.5:20; 2Ti.4:2; Tit.2:15.

to shape our hearts. This takes a concerted effort by the church family working together to help each other. We are to encourage one another in a life of purity. We are to gently rebuke one another when one evidences unrepentant sin.[50] It's like a teammate trying to help another struggling player to do better. As the family of God, we are there for one another. We understand that we are one body, one team, working together to help the entire body or team accomplish its goal. No person should be left behind, and no single person should stand alone.

To Evangelize the World. God teaches that we are to share the good new of Jesus Christ with the world so that all can partake in the forgiveness, purpose and hope that God offers.[51] It seems silly to have to instruct God's people to share the good news with others. If you had something fantastic to offer to someone else, surely you would be actively trying to get that good news out to everyone you knew. Why wouldn't a Christian want to share the absolutely amazing good news of Jesus Christ with others? Yet, because it is so easy to be beaten down by persecution or of simply not being heard, God has reminded us of our great commission to share the spiritual good news with others.

To Stabilize the World. God teaches that the Christian is to have an affect on the world. We are called the "salt of the world."[52] In the ancient world salt was used to preserve and flavor food. There was no refrigeration so salt was used. The world can be a crazy place with fads and selfish indulgence that make it difficult to see life through God's eyes. Christian values and teachings are anchored in God's nature, as described in the Bible, which does not change with the latest fad. The Bible contains tried and true solid life teachings and perspectives of life that span all cultures and all times.

Salt was also used, and still is, to add flavor to food. In like manner Christians add flavor to life. It should be the flavor of

---

[50] Lk.17:3.
[51] Mt.28:18-20; Mk.16:15; 1Ti.4:2; Ro.10:14-15.
[52] Mt.5:13; Mk.9:50; Lk.14:34.

humility, honesty, care, love, courage, and service. One Christian living this type of life will have an impact on those around him or her and thereby flavor the lives of all who are touched by this life.

To Benevolize the World. I made up this word to rhyme with the others listed above (an old preacher tactic). My intent is to emphasize the "benevolent" nature of God's people. God teaches that the church is to help others who are less fortunate.[53] In Matthew 25:34-46 Jesus describes a scene of judgment in which there are dire consequences for failure to help people in need and great reward for those who do help.

The church is not simply a gathering of Christians for their own enjoyment. It is a team of Christians working together to accomplish God's purposes. However, upon carrying out the work of God, Christians find the joy, excitement and victory that grows out of being a part of a winning team or a "band of brothers." There is no more important work in life than that of the work of God and his church. There is no better way *to be* built up - than to build others up for Christ's sake.

We may at times be sidelined by some hardship, but this should typically be temporary in nature. We are part of a team and no team member is expected to sit permanently on the bench as simply a spectator. Although injury, illness, financial distress, or age may affect how we can serve, we can all serve. Some have the greatest impact on others when they serve during their own personal hardship. With knowledge, wisdom and experience, some do their greatest work in old age.

Church is about love, encouragement and service. Church is about teamwork. It is God's desire that we all engage with his church.

> [24]And let us consider how we may spur one another on toward love and good deeds. [25]Let us not give up meeting

---

[53] Gal.6:10; Heb.13:16.

together, as some are in the habit of doing, but let us encourage one another.[54]

The church is part of that *full abundant eternal* life promised by Jesus. It is a force in shaping each of us into what we can only be with God's help. It is an essential element of God's plan to bring people into his eternal family and in helping them to make it through the challenges of life.

Transition to Heaven

Eternal life then continues on for eternity. The final stage of that eternal abundant life is heaven, the eternal dwelling place of God. The biblical picture of heaven is somewhat cryptic and it is difficult to know for certain how to interpret some of the visionary imagery, especially in the apocalyptic books like Revelation. The biblical authors are trying to describe something beyond our ability to fully understand. We are humans trapped in a physical world trying to understand spiritual truths.

Additionally, the apocalyptic style of writing, so common during the writing of the New Testament documents, has been lost to the world for almost 2,000 years. You can just imagine how difficult it would be for someone in the 41st century to try to interpret our newspaper political cartoons of the 21st century if political cartoons had not been used for 2,000 years and the 41st century readers were uncertain of the facts underlying the cartoons.

As such, a variety of theories exist on the events that will bring us from this present physical world to the eternal heavenly home of God.[55] Personally I don't think it matters which interpretation

---

[54] Heb.10:24-25.

[55] *End Times.* Revelation 20 describes a 1,000-year reign of Christ, the destruction of Satan, and the judgment of the dead. There are three primary ways in which Christians interpret Revelation 20. Premillennialists hold

Christians hold regarding these events. What is important is the life we live now. We need to unite with Christ, allow God to lead, and commit to being God's servants here on earth.[56] The rest will flow naturally.

There are some aspects of the transition from this life to the next that hold a large consensus. When Jesus ascended to heaven after his resurrection from the dead angels told the disciples, "This same Jesus, who has been taken from you into heaven, will come back in the same way you have seen him go into heaven."[57] Later the Apostle Paul also spoke about the Lord's second coming. He uses the term "sleep" as a euphemism for "death."

> [13]Brothers, we do not want you to be ignorant about those who fall asleep, or to grieve like the rest of men, who have no hope. [14]We believe that Jesus died and rose again and so we believe that God will bring with Jesus those who have fallen asleep in him. [15]According to the Lord's own word, we tell you that we who are still alive, who are left till the coming of the Lord, will certainly not precede

---

that Jesus will physically return to the earth to reign for 1,000 years during the golden age of peace while Satan is restrained. Postmillennialists hold that Jesus will return after the 1,000 year golden age of peace. Amillennialists hold that the 1,000 years described in Revelation 20 is a symbolic or figurative number and not meant to be taken literally. They typically hold Christ's reign began when the church started in about AD 30 and that Christ will return at some appointed time in the future.

[56] *Interpretation.* Many doctrinal controversies have no life decision consequences. For instance, people who believe the earth was created in millions of years can live the same life of holiness as those who believe the earth was created in 6 days (24 hour periods). Those who believe in the restoration of a physical earth at the end of time can live the same life of holiness as those who believe our final stage of life will be spiritual and not physical. Rather, the important doctrinal controversies that impact our lives are the ones that affect the choices we make in morality, service, and commitment to God while here in this physical life.

[57] Ac.1:11.

those who have fallen asleep. [16]For the Lord himself will come down from heaven, with a loud command, with the voice of the archangel and with the trumpet call of God, and the dead in Christ will rise first. [17]After that, we who are still alive and are left will be caught up together with them in the clouds to meet the Lord in the air. And so we will be with the Lord forever. [18]Therefore encourage each other with these words.[58]

Our Heavenly Home

God has given us insight into our heavenly home. The Bible does not support the popular picture of heaven with winged angels sitting on clouds and strumming harps. The harps that are pictured are described as being played by the 24 elders at the throne of God,[59] and by the people who persevered and are welcomed into heaven.[60] The Apostle, Peter, is never described in the Bible as waiting at the gate of heaven to interview newcomers.

What we can say with certainty is that heaven is the dwelling place of God.[61] For those who love and want to be with God, heaven is where we want to be. It is God's own home. It will be like coming home after being away for a long time. It's like seeing a familiar

---

[58] 1Th.4:13-18 ."*Rapture*" is a term used to describe the Lord's return to gather his people. Again we have differences of opinion about how the Lord's return will occur. Pre-tribulationists believe the Lord will meet one group of people in the air and leave another group of people behind on earth. The popular "Left Behind" series in book and film follow this approach. The other view simply holds that Paul is making a general reference to the final resurrection. This second view does not hold a second group will be left behind on earth.

[59] Rev.5:8.

[60] Rev.14:2; 15:2.

[61] Dt.26:15; 1 Ki.8:30; 2 Chron.30:27; Ps.123:1; Ac.7:48-49.

friendly face we have longed for. Spending eternity with the God we love is a wonderful thought.

We must make an *affirmative* decision to choose God in order to see God's home.[62] Christ will lead his followers to the home of God where they will be welcomed as adopted children. Heaven is where those who choose God will spend their eternity.[63] It is here where Christ has prepared a place designed specifically for us.[64] Heaven is a type of spiritual restoration of the biblical picture of the Garden of Eden.

The last book of the Bible describes the coming New Jerusalem.[65] Some view this in physical terms with God coming to earth, restoring the physical earth, and creating a heaven on earth. Others view this language in figurative terms as a way to describe certain physical events leading up to final spiritual heaven. *Some* of the

---

[62] Jn.1:12-13; Ro.10:12.

[63] Mt.16:19-21; Lk.10:17-20; 2Co.5:1.

[64] Jn.14:2-3.

[65] *New heaven and new earth.* The picture in Revelation 21-22 is of a City, called ""a new heaven and a new earth" (Rev.21:1), "the Holy City" (Rev.21:2), "the new Jerusalem" (Rev.21:2), and "the Holy City, Jerusalem" (Rev.21:10). This is the City where God lives (Rev.21:3). It is the dwelling place of God – the fundamental quality of heaven (1 Ki.8:27; Am.9:6; Ac.7:55). The Book of Revelation is written in what is known as "apocalyptic" style. This is a peculiar genre of literature that has been dead since the 2nd century AD. This amazing book has given rise to four primary methods of interpreting its dynamic imagery. (1) The Historist sees this as "prophecy about church history from the time of John to the end of the world." (2) The Preterist sees this as "prophecy that was fulfilled primarily in the first century AD." (3) The Futurist sees this as "prophecy primarily about the future end of the world." (4) The Idealist sees this as "a non-historical and non-prophetic drama about spiritual realities." *Understanding the Book of Revelation*, Torrance, CA: Rose Publishing, 2009, p.1. Although there are several different ways to interpret the images of Revelation, each perspective is inspiring and strengthening to the reader who sees God at work in the message. Regardless of the interpretive view one holds of Revelation, there is complete agreement on the practical message of the book. Tough times will challenge us, but if we persevere and remain true to God, we will be victorious with Christ and live in paradise.

imagery of Revelation is identified as figurative and it's meaning is expressly revealed.[66] So the question is whether the rest of the book is to be understood as a *literal* or a *figurative* description of events? Even with the uncertainty of many of the images, there are descriptions of this heavenly New Jerusalem, aka heaven, to which we faithfully cling with hope and confidence.

There will be no more sin in heaven.[67] As such, the ugliness and pain caused by sin will not reside in heaven. Those of us in Christ, who are presently in process of being changed into what we can be, will complete the task of transformation at the time of our calling to God's heavenly home.[68] I think it's a bit like the way my computer sometimes downloads updates and programs. I watch the download bar slowly move to the right as the updated file is slowly received. Sometimes it even appears stuck for a short time. It moves to the far right, and then, as if in the blink of an eye, it seems to just complete the process and it is done. Paul explains the change from our present form to that of our heavenly form in this way,

> [51]Listen, I tell you a mystery: We will not all sleep, but we will all be changed— [52]in a flash, in the twinkling of an eye, at the last trumpet. For the trumpet will sound, the dead will be raised imperishable, and we will be changed.[69]

Heaven truly will be a wonderful place. We will not die.[70] There will be no more hunger.[71] There will be no more tears.[72] There will no more exhaustion.[73] There is a spring with water so that none

---

[66] Rev.1:20; 4:5; 5:6; 11:8; 12:9; 17:9-12; 17:18.
[67] Rev.21:27.
[68] Phl.1:6; Ja.1:4; 1Jn.3:2.
[69] 1Co.15:51-52.
[70] Lk.20:36; 1Co.15:26, 54; 2Ti.1:10; Rev.21:4.
[71] Rev.7:16-17.
[72] Rev.21:4.
[73] Rev.14:13.

will be thirsty.[74] The Tree of Life that was lost in the Garden of Eden appears again.[75] God resides with people in this picture of perfect living.[76] There are some significant parallels between the picture of the Garden of Eden and the picture of the New Jerusalem.[77]

I envision heaven as a place of joyous celebration. The Kingdom of God is about righteousness, peace and joy.[78] We will be filled with joy in God's presence.[79] How could such a wonderful setting be anything but joyous?

Our Heavenly Bodies

New eternal bodies will eventually replace our present physical bodies. The Apostle Paul called these two bodies the present "perishable...natural body" verses the new "imperishable...spiritual body."[80] He tried to explain the difference between the temporary physical body and the eternal spiritual body in 1 Corinthians 15,[81] but he struggled to express what will never make full sense while we live a physical existence.

Our new bodies will be glorious and not fraught with the problems of our frail physical bodies.[82] They may or may not be revised, renewed or healed version of our present bodies. Some of us are born with physical problems. Some are very serious. Almost all of us grow into an increasing set of physical problems as we age.

---

74 Rev.21:6.

75 Rev.22:2.

76 Rev.21:3

77 *Garden & New Jerusalem.* There are also some obvious differences between the picture of the Garden of Eden and the New Jerusalem. One is a natural garden and the other is a city.

78 Ro.14:7.

79 Ps.16:11.

80 1Co.15:44.

81 1Co.15:35-58.

82 1Co.15:35-54.

Eventually our physical bodies are struck down by disease, trauma, or wear and tear. The Bible tells us our new bodies will never wear out. They will be imperishable.[83]

In heaven we will live without marriage, like the angels.[84] Although this may at first appear undesirable, the underlying theme is that we will be so connected to God and possibly others, that we will have no need of the marriage type relationship. We will not have the *physical* needs of marriage and the social needs will be met by the spiritual relationships we will have in heaven.

Being with and Recognizing Others in Heaven

Many believe we will be able to recognize each other in heaven. There is no clear statement in the Bible, but certain events *may* give rise to an *inference* that the resurrected body is recognizable. One day Peter, James, and John accompanied Jesus up a high mountain. Upon reaching the top Jesus was dramatically changed. His face shown bright like the sun and his clothes became whiter than any clothes possible. Moses and Elijah, who had passed away hundreds of years before, appeared with Jesus in "glorious splendor." Moses and Elijah were talking with Jesus. Peter was excited, and in an effort to honor them, suggested that they build three simple shelters – one for each transfigured man of faith. Before he could take any action a cloud enveloped them and a voice from the cloud said, "This is my Son, whom I love. Listen to him!" The disciples fell to the ground in homage to God's voice. When they looked up, they saw only Jesus.[85]

Jesus' body was transformed before the eyes of his disciples into what might be deemed a glimpse of his heavenly form. "His face shown like the sun, and his clothes became as white as the

---

[83] 1Co.15:42.

[84] Lk.20:35.

[85] Mt.17:1-8; Mk.9:2-8; Lk.9:28-36.

light."[86] "His clothes became dazzling white, whiter than anyone in the world could bleach them."[87] Moses and Elijah "appeared in glorious splendor."[88] The disciples appear to have recognized Moses and Elijah even though they had never met them and had never seen a picture of them. Somehow they knew the identity of these two prophets of old. The disciples also recognized Jesus in his transfigured form. In comparing God's people with Jesus, Paul writes, "As is the man from heaven, so also are those who are of heaven."[89] Thus we *may* be able to *infer* that our heavenly bodies will be recognizable.

There are a number of passages in the Bible that indicate we will gather with others throughout time.[90] What an amazing thought. I may be able to meet with and interact with not only members of my own family who have already gone on to meet the Lord, but also the great faith giants from the past. We will all be part of that adopted family of God.

The Importance of Heaven

It is enticing to think about heaven. We don't know many details, and some of what we read is difficult to interpret and understand. But what we do know is that heaven is the existence we want for eternity. It is God's home with a place prepared especially for us. How could anyone who loves God not long to be invited to God's own home? Here we will come to know God immensely better than we ever could while traveling on this physical earth.[91]

---

[86] Mt.17:2.
[87] Mk.9:3.
[88] Lk.9:30-31.
[89] 1Co.15:48.
[90] 2Sa.12:23; Mt.8:11.
[91] 1Co.13:12.

This realization provides strength as we face the challenges of life. Our present struggles pale in comparison to the beauty, wonder and brilliance of heaven.[92] This knowledge is incentive to remain true to God and make it through the hurdles of life to obtain the wonders of God. We know that all of God's people comprising the family of God in heaven are pulling for us in life.[93] This makes the difficulties of this life bearable. The knowledge and hope of heaven help us live the victorious holy life of God in difficult situations. Heaven is a wonderful hope.

My Home

My home is nothing fancy. For the average American my house is certainly not big, upper scale, or high end. It's just a small nicely furnished and cared for single-family dwelling in the San Francisco Bay Area. We have a two-car garage, a little grass out front, a patio outside the family room French doors, and beyond that a small built-in pool and some grass (when the drought doesn't kill it off). My house is one of a host of houses built more than a generation ago. The neighborhood street in front is lightly traveled with owners going here and there to make their way to work or run errands. The same builder built almost every other house in the blocks surrounding my house. They are all simply variations of the same basic floor plan.

A good portion of my life is spent away from our house. I work a full business week at an office some distance from home. I work in trust, conservatorship, and estate administration. As with most jobs, there are fun, exciting, and meaningful parts of my work. I love my fellow employees. We work well together. Most of us working in my department have been working together for a number of years. We commiserate together, laugh together, and rely on each other's

---

[92] 2Co.4:16-17.
[93] Heb.12:1-3.

help and expertise. We also share times together outside of normal working activities. We have shared lunch and dinners, attended shows, and participated in other events that are not directly related to my employment, except as a networking tool.

Like every job, there are also uncomfortable or disagreeable times. Sometimes we have disgruntled beneficiaries who simply can't appreciate the intensity and quality of work put forth on their behalf. Sometimes procedural paperwork consumes an inordinate amount of time and effort for very little value or return. Sometimes there is just too much work to get done and tough deadlines that create an uncomfortable urgency.

Arriving at home after a typical day of work feels good. My wife and dogs are there to greet me. I can relax in my own comfortable setting. The house has been shaped to fit me, my wife, and our needs and desires. Our furniture is the type of furniture we find comfortable. The paint is in the colors that make us happy. The temperature is set at a comfortable level for us. The food is the type of food that we enjoy eating – perhaps too much! This is our home shaped to fit our personalities and needs.

When I get to the end of my workday I look forward to the comfort and relaxation at home. When the time comes to pack up my office, there is a rush of excitement. I then close the door to my office, walk out of the company door, take the elevator or stairs down to the ground floor, climb into my car hidden in the underground parking garage, and head on home.

The strange thing is that even if I have had a fantastic day, or been on a wonderful trip, home always feels good. I enjoy working, traveling and experiencing new adventures, but home is special. When Dorothy says in the Wizard of Oz, "There is no place like home,"[94] she is echoing what I typically feel.

---

[94] *The Wizard of Oz* is a 1939 American musical fantasy film produced by Metro-Goldwyn-Mayer, and the most well-known and commercially successful adaptation based on the 1900 novel *The Wonderful Wizard*

As comfortable as my home is, it is not perfect. Anyone who owns a home knows that the maintenance never stops. There is always something to fix. Last year our kitchen oven went out and our stovetop was on its last legs. So we decided to spend the money to replace the stovetop and oven. Unfortunately, while they were installing the new stovetop and oven, we learned that we had to upgrade our electrical supply box to provide the necessary power to our new appliances. So we spent more money. In the process of replacing that electrical box we discovered the roof had serious problems and would probably leak at the next big rain. So we bit the bullet and put on a new roof. One would hope that spending that kind of money would fix everything – but it didn't. We have replaced most of the fence and one gate, and are still working on another gate. Then we need to replace the lamppost out front. As soon as we get that done, there will be a list of new items that need work.

Additionally, my house isn't as secure and safe as I sometimes think or would like to think. One day my wife was at home by herself when she heard our dogs barking. As she peered through the shutters she saw a bunch of police cars, policemen, and our neighbor talking to one of the officers. Our neighbor called and Sharon was told to stay in the house with the dogs. A policeman came over, introduced himself and then explained that there had been three men who had broken into a house behind ours while a teenage girl was there. She had escaped and called 911 and the police were searching back yards house by house to find these men who were trying to get away. They searched our yard, left one officer in the yard, and other officers moved on to the next house. One neighbor estimated there were about 40 police cars around our block. Apparently this was a gang of burglars the police had been trying to find for some time and now they had them within their grasp. They found two of the men hiding in a yard behind ours. A police dog eventually discovered the third burglar hiding in a neighbor's yard down the street. "Ouch!"

Like our physical lives, our spiritual life's journey is filled with experiences both good and bad. Sometimes it is fun, meaningful, exciting and enjoyable. At other times it is filled with challenges, and mean, vicious, and uncaring people. Sometimes life is so difficult we wonder how we will be able to continue. In spite of the challenges most of us do continue on. God provides the strength to not only continue on, but to continue on with a life of holiness, regardless of the circumstances.

God's home (heaven) is our home with a place created especially for each of us. It fits us. It provides us what we need. It will be meaningful, exciting and enjoyable. However, unlike my physical home, my heavenly home will not deteriorate or require constant maintenance. It will be fully safe and secure and I won't have to worry about burglars or worse. Heaven will have the comfort of home, the love of family, the brightness of day, the beauty of life, and the security of God's protection. This is where "everlasting life" comes to fruition.

Summary

Eternal life is the full abundant life that begins with our commitment to Christ and goes on for eternity. It is a life that will find its permanent home with God in heaven. Our heavenly home is created specifically for our needs and us. It's a haven of safety, peace, and love.

Thought Questions

1. What does "everlasting life" mean to you?

2. What does "the abundant life" mean to you?

3. What do you think heaven will be like?

4. Do you look forward to living with God in heaven? Why or why not?

5. Is it worth it to turn your life over to God to obtain everlasting life and the chance for heaven? Why or why not?

12

Epilogue

A Fantastic Story

It is truly a fantastic story. Could it all possibly be true? After all, this is not the type of stuff we see in everyday life. Or is it?

Billions of people over time have been led and motivated to give selflessly to others and to persevere in the toughest of circumstances because of their love and allegiance to God through Jesus Christ. Some of the great civil rights movements of the past were led by people who were committed to Christ Jesus, like William Wilberforce and Martin Luther King, Jr. Some of those most dedicated to the poor and helpless were acting out of a love for Christ Jesus, like Sister Teresa.

Some of those with the greatest courage were led by their allegiance to Christ Jesus, like Francis of Assisi who went individually to the Muslim Sultan to try to convert him in the middle of the Crusades. It is a David Wilkerson who walked into the territory of some very dangerous gangs to teach gang members like Nicki Cruz about Jesus. It is people of selfless service like Father Damien who went to the island of Molokai to work with lepers knowing he would eventually die of the disease himself all because of his love for Christ.

I am one of those people touched by this amazing story and by my relationship with God. Do I hear booming voices from heaven? No, it is more like a quiet inner voice. Have I seen a parting of the sea? No, but I have seen insurmountable odds overcome by incredible sacrificial giving motivated by faith in God. Have I seen lepers restored to health? No, but I have seen broken relationships restored and dramatic recoveries from cancer. I have seen people addicted to drugs find Christ and victory in life. Have I ever seen an angel? Not that I could recognize, but I have seen a child get hit by a car, fly high in the air, flip and land on the asphalt road, with only a few bruises to show for it, as if an invisible angel had caught the child and cushioned his fall. I have seen the change of heart that has come upon others and myself that arises from the commitment to Christ Jesus. It is evident to me that God's work is happening all around us all the time. All we have to do is open our eyes to see it.

John 3:16

So there you have it. One verse. One sentence. And yet it is packed with depth that is almost unfathomable. John 3:16 is the message of Christianity. The core and heart of the entire Bible is right here.

I have now been a Christian for decades. I have seen hypocrites clothed in the disguise of Christianity. I fear at times I may have been one of those hypocrites. I have also seen Christians with unbelievable courage and compassion. I have personally witnessed and been astounded by those who selflessly gave of themselves and their resources to help others who were struggling. I have been the recipient of unfair, mean and vicious criticism. I have also been the recipient of compassion, praise and respect. I have been let down by some people and amazed by the strength and dependability of others. This is the way life is – filled with bad and good. But through it all, we have a God who always loves us. This is our rock!

Love is the reason for the existence of people. Love is the motive that brought Jesus to the earth in physical form. Love is the reason for Jesus to endure the horrific sacrifice. Love is why there was a plan in the first place. Love is why there is hope for the future. Love is the reason for all of it.

So what? Ask yourself, "What difference does this passage or this thought make in my life? Does anything change as a result of it? Am I a different person because of it?" For me the answer is, "Yes, definitely. It helps me understand life. It motivates, focuses and energizes me. It brings me closer to God."

Spend time with this passage. One could meditate, study and pray through the various parts of this passage for a lifetime and never discover its full depth. I read this verse, shared this verse, and taught this verse many times before I even thought of writing this book. I have spent countless hours studying and meditating on this passage as I prepared this book for publication. With each new discovery, this passage becomes richer than it was before.

For almost two thousand years, this passage has been a favorite. There is a reason for that. This simple verse captures the nature of God and the hope offered to us as nothing else does. Take lasting encouragement from these simple words.

> *For God so loved the world, that he gave his one and only Son, that whoever believes in him shall not perish but have everlasting life.*

Glossary of Church Words

Atonement: To make amends for wrongdoing. Atonement for sin can only be made by the shedding of blood (Heb.9:22). The Israelites sacrificed animals to make atonement (Lev.17:11). It is the blood of Jesus that truly accomplishes atonement (Heb.10:4; Mt.26:28; Ro.5:9; heb.9:14; 1Pe.1:18-19; 1 Jn.1:7; Rev.1:5).

Blasphemy: The *life* decision *not* to acknowledge and follow God. The original Greek term was akin to our "defamation." However, in a religious sense it took on the meaning of refusing to acknowledge and respect God as God. There is only one unforgivable sin – rejection of God and His good news. This is an *attitude* problem. This shows itself in blatant repeated sin (Nu.15:30-31; 1 Jn.3:6). The one unforgiveable sin is called "blasphemy of the Holy Spirit," because it is rejection of the Holy Spirit, who is the last witness to our hearts of God's good news (Mk.3:28-29). Blasphemy arises out of a heart that refuses to follow God.

Born Again: Being transformed into a person with new attitudes, perspectives and approach to life by one's commitment to Christ and the indwelling of the Holy Spirit (Jn.3:3-8; Rom.12:1-2; Gal.5:16-26; Col.3:1-17).

Canon: The collection of writings accepted by an official Christian authority, such as a Church council, as Scripture and authored by God. The Old Testament was accepted as God's work as it was created. The Old Testament was fully formed 400 years prior to the coming of Jesus. The writings of the apostles were immediately deemed to be Scripture in the same sense (2Pe.3:16). Lists of recognized divine writings that would eventually form our New Testament began to develop as early as AD 95, but these were not meant to be complete lists. In AD 367 Athanasius, Bishop of Alexandria, wrote a letter that included a listing of the 27 books he believed had been accepted by Christians as New Testament Scripture. In 393 The Synod of Hippo approved the 27 books of the New Testament. The Council of Carthage (397) also approved the 27 books of the New Testament.

Church: (*ekklesia* "assembly") The people called out to meet together for God. The Church meets together to encourage, strengthen and love one another (Heb.10:24-25). It is called the "body of Christ" made up of many different kinds of members each with an important function (1Co.12:12-27). The Church has one head, who is Christ (Eph.4:15).

Consecrate: The process of dedicating or committing something or someone to God.

Eternal Life: The full abundant forever life, which begins upon making a commitment to Christ, and lasts for eternity. Physical death is just a transformation from one stage of life to another – like the way life moves from fetus to infant or from a caterpillar to a butterfly. (Jn.3:36; 4:14; 5:24; 6:40-47; 10:10; 11:25)

Faith: Belief, trust, <u>dependence</u>. Faith coupled with Grace is key to salvation. (Ro.3:21-24; Eph.2:8)

Forgiveness: Refraining from demanding justice, and instead treating the person *as if* he/she had not acted wrongfully. Jesus died to pay the sentence and debt owed by each of us. The wrongdoer's sin is completely forgiven upon uniting with Christ in faith. All further sin will be forgiven as long as the wrongdoer repents of any sin committed and recommits to God's leadership.

Grace: A gift, as opposed to something earned or deserved. God's Riches At Christ's Expense. Grace is God's *gift* of forgiveness and life. Grace coupled with Faith is key to salvation. (Ro.2:8)

Heaven: The dwelling place of God and the eternal realm of those who chose to walk with God during physical life. (Dt.26:15; 1 Ki.8:30; 2 Ch.30:27; Job.22:12; Ps.73:25; 103:19; 123:1; Isa.66:1; Lk.11:2; Ac.7:49)

Hell: The absence of God and the place of the spirits of the dead who chose *not* to walk with God during physical life. It is pictured as a place of fire and thirst to be avoided at all costs. (Mt.25:46; Lk.16:23)

Holy: Set apart from the common and dedicated to God's purposes. God's people are Holy if they are set apart for God's purposes. (1Pe.2:9)

Holy Spirit: God's Spirit, breath or essence which indwells Christians (Ro.8:9). God gives us a part of himself to live within us and to meld with our own spirit (1Co.2). However, God's Spirit can be resisted or squelched.

Justification: Making the balance even. No outstanding debt.

Redemption: To regain or obtain possession of something by giving something, other than money, in exchange. Jesus redeemed us before God by hanging on the cross and suffering in our place.

Righteous(ness): Rightness, measured by God's perfection (Mt.5:48). There are none righteous by themselves. (Ro.3:10)

Sanctification: The process of making someone holy. Comes from the same original Hebrew and Greek root term as "holy." Jesus' death on the cross and the indwelling of the Holy Spirit are at work in the sanctification of the Christian.

Scripture: The Old Testament and New Testament of the Bible. Documents identified as inspired by divine revelation.

Sin: Missing the mark. Not measuring up to God's glorious ideal of what life should and can look like (Ro.3:23). Sin includes the breaking of God's commandments (1 Jn.3:4). Sin includes both acts of commission and acts of omission (Ja.4:17). Sin is not only the breaking of a rule or law. At its most basic level, sin is not being what God wants us to be. Our sin separates us from God. (Isa.59:1-2; Ro.3:10-18; 6:23)

Tithe: Giving the first or best $1/10^{th}$ of one's income or goods as a gift to God or His work. In the Old Testament the required giving began with $1/10^{th}$ as a base. Depending on circumstances, one could be required to give much more. In the New Testament, the amount is determined by the joyful giving heart and not a set percentage (Mt.10:8; 2Co.9:7)

Worship: Dedication, awe, respect and service to some being or thing. Christian worship is full and complete dedication to the God of the Bible through Jesus Christ (Ro.12:1-2; Jn.4:21-24). It is recognition that Jesus is the only way to truly reach God (Jn.14:6; Ac.4:12).

Bibliography

Books

Aland, Kurt; Black, Matthew; Martini, Carlo M.; Metzger, Bruce M.; Wikgren, Allen, Editors. *The Greek New Testament*, 3rd ed. West Germany: United Bible Societies, 1983.

Bruce, F.F., *The Canon of Scripture*. Downers Grove, IL: InterVarsity Press, 1988.

Douglas, J.D., Editor. *Dictionary of the Christian Church*. Grand Rapids, Michigan: Zondervan Publishing House, 1978, p.791.

Flew, Antony, *There Is A God*, Harper One: New York, New York, 2007.

Fudge, Edward, William, *Hell A Final Word*, Abilene, TX: Leafwood Publishers, 2012

Gingrich, F. Wilbur, Editor. *Shorter Lexicon of the Greek New Testament*. Chicago: The University of Chicago Press, 1965.

Isaacson, Walter, *Einstein, His Life and Universe*, New York, NY: Simon & Schuster, 2007.

Jones, Timothy Paul, Gundersen, David, & Galan, Benjamin, *End-Times Prophecy*, Torrance, CA: Rose Publishing, Inc., 2011

Lewis, C.S., *The Four Loves,* Boston & New York: Mariner Books, 1960, Kindle Ed.

Lightfoot, Neil R. *How We Got the Bible*, Grand Rapids, MI: Baker Book House, 1963

Marshall, Alfred, Editor. *The NIV Interlinear Greek-English New Testament.* Grand Rapids, Mich: Zondervan Corp. 1976.

Metzger, Bruce, *The Text of the New Testament*, New York & Oxford: Oxford University Press, 1968.

Petersen, Carolyn Collins, *Astronomy 101*, Avon, MA: Adams Media, 2013.

Phillips, John. *Exploring the Gospel of John.* Grand Rapids, MI: Kregel Publications (1989).

Scorgie, Glen G., Staruss, Mark L., Voth, Steven M., *The Challenge of Bible Translation*, Grand Rapids, MI: Zondervan, 2003.

Strobel, Lee, *The Case For A Creator,* by Lee Strobel, Zondervan: Grand Rapids, Michigan, 2004.

Strong, James, Editor. *The New Strong's Expanded Dictionary of Bible Words.* Nashville: Thomas Nelson Publishers, 2001.

Thomas, Robert L. & Gundry, Stanley N., *The NIV Harmony of the Gospels*, New York, NY: Harper Collins Publishers, 1988.

Zerwick, Max & Grosvenor, Mary. *A Grammatical Analysis of the Greek New Testament.* Rome: Biblical Institute Press, 1974.

Periodicals

Mykytiuk, Lawrence, *Biblical Archaeology Review*, Vol.41, No.1, Washington, DC: Biblical Archaeology Society, 2014, *Did Jesus Exist?*, pp.1C 61.

Encyclopedias, Dictionaries & Compilations

Chronological and Background Charts of the New Testament. Grand Rapids: Zondervan Publishing House, 1981 p.76

Famous Statements Speeches & Stories of Abraham Lincoln, ed. & published by J. Donald Hawkins, 1991.

Shakespeare The Complete Works, Ed by G.B. Harrison, New York, Harcourt, Brace & World, Inc., 1968.

The International Standard Bible Encyclopaedia, Vol.IV. Grand Rapids, MI: Wm B. Eerdmans Publishing Co., 1956.

The Yale Book of Quotations, ed. by Fred R. Shapiro, New Haven & London: Yale University Press, 2006.

World Atlas online at http://www.worldatlas.com/nations.htm

Word Biblical Commentary, John, Vol.36, George R. Beasley-Murray, Nashville, TN; Thomas Nelson Publishers, 1999.

Music

Black, Clint. *Something That We Do*. One song on the *Nothing But the Taillights* album by RCA 1997.

Phelps, David. *End of the Beginning,* on *The Best of David Phelps* album released Mar.18, 2011, Spring House Music Group, EMI Christian Music Group.

Online

Bible, online at Wikipedia online at http://en.wikipedia.org/wiki/ Bible.

Blood Type, online at http://en.wikipedia.org/wiki/Blood_type.

Demographic History of Jerusalem, online at http://en.wikipedia. org/wiki/Demographic_history_of_Jerusalem.

DNA survey finds all humans are 99.9pc the same, by Roger Highfield, The Telegraph, 2002, online at http://www.telegraph.co.uk/news/ worldnews/northamerica/usa/1416706/DNA-survey-finds-all-humans-are-99.9pc-the-same.html

Earth Physical Characteristics Table, online at http://en.wikipedia. org/wiki/Earth_physical_characteristics_tables.

First Inauguration of Franklin D. Roosevelt, online at http://en.wikipedia.org/wiki/ First_inauguration_of_Franklin_D._Roosevelt.

I have a dream, online at http://en.wikipedia.org/ wiki/I_Have_a_Dream.

Inaugural Address by President John F Kennedy, January 20, 1961, online at http://en.wikipedia.org/wiki/Inauguration_of_John_F._Kennedy

InfoPlease online at http://www.infoplease.com/ipa/A0932875.html

John 3:16. Online at http://en.wikipedia.org/wiki/John_3:16. January 20, 2014.

John, the Apostle, Online at http://en.wikipedia.org/wiki/John_the_Apostle.

Josephus, *Wars*, Book 2, 21:5, cited in the *Life of Jesus Christ*, online at http://www.jesus-story.net/scourging.htm.

Love Big Island Blog online at http://www.lovebigisland.com/hawaii-blog/climate-zones-big-island/.

Major Religious Groups. Online at *http://en.wikipedia.org/wiki/Major_religious_groups.* February 13, 2014.

Play it Forward. Online at http://en.wikipedia.org/wiki/Pay_it_forward. February 19, 2014.

Thallus. Online at http://en.wikipedia.org/wiki/Thallus_(historian). February 19, 2014.

Wizard of Oz, Wikipedia online at http://en.wikipedia.org/wiki/The_Wizard_of_Oz_(1939_film).

Software

The Bible, New International Version. Quickverse software ver.3.0.0(119), 2009.

Index

S

W